NICE

Travel Guide 2025

Discover Timeless Charm And Vibrant Life on the French Riviera

CHARLES S. SIMONS

Copyright © 2025 Charles S. Simons. All Rights Reserved.

This guidebook is designed to provide up-to-date and reliable travel information for visitors to Nice. However, despite our best efforts to ensure accuracy, changes may occur after publication. Hotels may change ownership, restaurants might adjust their prices, museums could modify their opening hours, and transportation routes may be altered. While we strive to keep information current, we cannot be held responsible for any errors, omissions, or inconveniences resulting from changes that take place after this guide has been published.

By purchasing and downloading this book through authorized channels, you acknowledge and respect intellectual property laws. Unauthorized reproduction, modification, or distribution of this book, in whole or in part, is strictly prohibited.

We encourage travelers to double-check important details, such as operating hours, entry requirements, and transportation schedules, before making final plans.

Thank you for choosing our guidebook. We hope you have an amazing journey exploring Nice!

TABLE OF CONTENT

WELCOME TO NICE 7
- Why Visit Nice in 2025? 9
- What Nice Is & What It Is Not (Setting Realistic Expectations) 11
- How This Guide Will Help You Make the Most of Your Trip 12

ESSENTIAL TRAVEL INFORMATION 14
- Entry & Visa Requirements for 2025 15
- Currency, Budgeting & Payment Tips (Including Hidden Costs) 16
- Best Time to Visit Nice (Weather, Crowds & Seasonal Highlights) 18
- Language & Useful French Phrases for Tourists 20

GETTING TO NICE 22
- Arriving by Air: Nice Côte d'Azur Airport Guide 23
- Getting to Nice by Train, Car, or Cruise Ship 25
- Eco-Friendly Travel to Nice (Train vs. Flight Comparisons) 27

Getting Around Nice 30
- Public Transportation: Trams, Buses & Ticketing 31
- Walking & Biking: The Best Way to Explore the City 34

WHERE TO STAY IN NICE 38
- Best Neighborhoods to Stay in Nice (Pros & Cons) 39
- Top Hotels for Every Budget (Luxury, Mid-Range & Budget) 43
- Alternative Stays: Airbnbs, Hostels & Eco-Friendly Lodging 44

TOP ATTRACTIONS & LANDMARKS 47
- The Promenade des Anglais: Nice's Most Famous Walk 48
- Exploring Vieux Nice (Old Town) – Must-See Spots & Hidden Gems . 49

Castle Hill (Colline du Château) – Views, History & Secret Corners ... 51

Nice's Best Museums & Cultural Experiences 53

NICE BEYOND THE TOURIST SPOTS 55

Local Markets, Secret Alleys & Hidden Cafés 56

Exploring Nice's Lesser-Known Neighborhoods 58

How to Experience the City Like a Local 60

BEACHES & COASTAL EXPERIENCES 62

Public vs. Private Beaches: What to Expect 63

The Best Beaches for Swimming, Relaxing & Watersports 65

Beach Clubs, Sunbeds & Dining by the Water 66

OUTDOOR ADVENTURES & DAY TRIPS 70

The Best Hiking & Walking Trails Near Nice 71

Day Trips to Monaco, Cannes & Antibes 73

Hidden Villages & Off-the-Beaten-Path Excursions 75

FOOD & WINE IN NICE 78

Traditional Niçoise Dishes You Must Try 79

Best Restaurants for Every Budget 80

Wine, Cocktails & Riviera Drinks 82

Where to Find the Best Bakeries, Ice Cream & Coffee Shops 83

Special Diets: Vegetarian, Vegan & Gluten-Free Dining 83

SHOPPING & SOUVENIRS IN NICE 85

Where to Shop: Best Streets & Markets 86

Unique Souvenirs & Local Crafts 87

Luxury Shopping & Designer Boutiques 89

NICE'S NIGHTLIFE & ENTERTAINMENT 91

Rooftop Bars, Beachfront Lounges & Jazz Clubs 92

Casinos & Evening Shows 93

The Best Late-Night Experiences in Nice 93

FESTIVALS & EVENTS IN 2025 95

Nice Carnival: What to Expect & How to Experience It Best 96

Music, Food & Art Festivals Throughout the Year............................... 97

Sporting Events & Cultural Celebrations 99

NICE FOR EVERY TYPE OF TRAVELER 101

Family-Friendly Attractions & Activities 102

Romantic Getaways & Honeymoon Ideas... 103

Solo Travel & Social Spots 104

Budget Travel: How to Experience Nice for Less................................ 105

How to Travel Sustainably in Nice 109

Supporting Local Businesses & Ethical Tourism 110

Eco-Friendly Transport, Hotels & Dining Options 111

What's Overrated & What's Worth Your Time?................................. 115

Common Scams & How to Stay Safe in Nice 116

Mistakes First-Time Visitors Make & How to Avoid Them................ 118

PRACTICAL TRAVEL TIPS FOR A SMOOTH TRIP 120

Packing Tips & Essentials for Nice's Climate 121

Understanding Local Etiquette & Cultural Norms.............................. 122

Emergency Contacts, Health & Safety Information 123

Digital Traveler's Guide (Best Apps, WiFi, eSIMs & Useful Websites) 123

ITINERARIES FOR EVERY TYPE OF TRAVELER **126**

24-Hour Itinerary: Maximizing a Short Visit 127

3-Day Itinerary: The Perfect Weekend in Nice 129

7-Day Itinerary: A Relaxed Yet Complete Experience 130

Customizing Your Trip Based on Interests.. 133

FINAL THOUGHTS & INSIDER ADVICE **135**

A Local's Last Tips for the Best Experience....................................... 136

How to Leave Nice Without Regrets 137

Why You'll Want to Return.. 138

FREQUENTLY ASKED QUESTIONS **140**

1

WELCOME TO NICE

Step off the plane, train, or cruise ship, and you'll feel it instantly—the Mediterranean warmth, the soft scent of the sea mingling with freshly baked croissants, and the golden light dancing off the pastel-colored facades of Belle Époque buildings. Welcome to Nice, the jewel of the French Riviera, where time slows just enough for you to savor every sun-drenched moment.

Nice isn't just a destination; it's an experience, a feeling that lingers long after your footprints fade from the Promenade des Anglais. It's the rush of excitement as you weave through the labyrinthine alleys of Vieux Nice, the rhythmic hum of the waves against pebbled shores, the indulgence of a leisurely café crème at a sunlit terrace, and the awe of watching the sunset paint the sky in hues of rose and gold.

This city, perched gracefully between the Alps and the Mediterranean, wears many faces. It's a playground for artists, a haven for history lovers, and a paradise for food enthusiasts. One moment, you're admiring a Matisse masterpiece in a museum; the next, you're biting into a warm socca, a crispy chickpea pancake beloved by locals. Here, life is savored slowly, deliciously, and always with a touch of elegance.

But Nice is not just about what you see—it's about what you feel. The easygoing rhythm of the Niçois lifestyle is infectious. Mornings begin with a gentle stroll to the local boulangerie, where the scent of buttery pastries fills the air. Afternoons invite you to laze on a sunbed at a private beach club or meander through flower-filled plazas, where laughter spills from lively brasseries. And when night falls, whether you choose a romantic rooftop bar or a vibrant jazz club tucked away in the Old Town, you'll understand why visitors fall in love with Nice—and why they always return.

This is your gateway to the French Riviera, a place where history, culture, and seaside beauty converge in perfect harmony. Whether it's your first visit or your fifth, whether you're here for a whirlwind weekend or a long, lingering escape, Nice welcomes you with open arms and endless sunshine.

Why Visit Nice in 2025?

There has never been a better time to visit Nice than in 2025. As one of the most beloved cities on the French Riviera, Nice continues to evolve, offering travelers a seamless blend of old-world charm and modern elegance. Whether you're a first-time visitor eager to experience the Mediterranean magic or a seasoned traveler returning to rediscover its hidden gems, 2025 promises a fresh and enriched experience of Nice.

A City That Gets Better with Time

Nice has always been a city of reinvention. Each year, new restaurants, boutique hotels, and cultural events breathe fresh life into its streets, enhancing what is already a world-class destination. In 2025, you'll find updated infrastructure, a renewed focus on sustainable tourism, and exciting events that make a visit more rewarding than ever.

Unforgettable Climate & Natural Beauty

Nice enjoys a mild Mediterranean climate year-round, meaning sunshine is practically guaranteed no matter when you visit. Whether it's a summer escape with warm breezes and inviting beaches or a winter retreat where you can soak up the sun while the rest of Europe shivers, Nice offers an ideal setting for outdoor adventures, leisurely promenades, and breathtaking coastal views.

Exciting Events & Festivals in 2025

From the legendary Nice Carnival in February—one of Europe's most spectacular street festivals—to the star-studded Nice Jazz Festival in July, 2025 is packed with cultural events that bring the city to life. Whether you're drawn by world-class music, vibrant parades, or gourmet food festivals, there's always something happening in Nice.

Gastronomic Delights & Culinary Renaissance

Nice has long been a food lover's paradise, and 2025 is set to elevate its culinary scene even further. Expect an increased emphasis on local, sustainable cuisine, with new restaurants focusing on Niçois specialties such as socca, pissaladière, and salade niçoise while reinterpreting classic Mediterranean flavors in innovative ways. Food markets like Cours Saleya remain must-visit spots, bursting with the colors and scents of Provence.

A Perfect Gateway to the French Riviera

Nice is more than just a destination; it's a launchpad to explore the wonders of the Côte d'Azur. With its excellent transport connections, you can take effortless day trips to glamorous Monaco, artistic Saint-Paul-de-Vence, or even the lavender fields of Provence. Whether you want to bask in luxury or seek out hidden coastal gems, Nice is your ideal home base in 2025.

What Nice Is & What It Is Not (Setting Realistic Expectations)

It's easy to fall in love with Nice, but the best way to truly enjoy the city is to arrive with realistic expectations. This is not just a sun-drenched Riviera retreat—it's a place with a distinct character, local quirks, and a blend of elegance and everyday life.

What Nice IS:

☐ A Coastal Paradise with a City Pulse – Nice is both a stunning beachside escape and a lively cultural hub. It's a city where you can spend the morning at a museum, the afternoon at a café, and the evening dancing under the stars.

☐ Rich in History & Culture – From its Italian-influenced Old Town to its world-class museums (including the Matisse Museum and the Marc Chagall Museum), Nice is a city of art, heritage, and deep Mediterranean roots.

☐ A Foodie's Dream – Expect fresh seafood, Provençal delights, and vibrant market culture. From Michelin-starred dining to casual seaside eats, the food scene in Nice caters to every palate.

☐ Walkable & Well-Connected – With its compact layout, Nice is best explored on foot. But when you need to venture beyond, an efficient tram and bus network makes getting around easy.

☐ A Year-Round Destination – While summer is the peak season, spring and autumn are perfect for fewer crowds, and even in winter, the mild temperatures make it an attractive escape from colder climates.

What Nice is NOT:

☐ A White Sand Beach Destination – Unlike other Mediterranean getaways, Nice's beaches are pebble, not sand. While the crystal-clear waters are stunning, you may want to bring water shoes for comfort.

☐ A Cheap Destination – While more affordable than nearby Cannes or Monaco, Nice is still part of the French Riviera, meaning prices for dining, hotels, and activities can be on the higher side, especially during peak season.

☐ A Non-Touristy Escape – Nice is one of the most visited cities in France, so don't expect deserted streets or hidden beaches. That said, visiting in the off-season or exploring lesser-known areas can help you avoid the crowds.

☐ Only About Beaches – Many travelers assume Nice is just for seaside lounging, but the city offers so much more—including hiking trails, wine country excursions, historical landmarks, and one of France's best art scenes.

By understanding what Nice truly offers, you'll be able to appreciate its beauty without unrealistic expectations, ensuring a much more rewarding and stress-free trip.

How This Guide Will Help You Make the Most of Your Trip

With so much to see, taste, and experience, planning a trip to Nice can feel overwhelming. That's where this guide comes in—designed to be your ultimate travel companion, ensuring you don't just visit Nice, but experience it in the best way possible.

What You Can Expect from This Guide:

✔ Comprehensive Insights – From the city's top attractions to its best-kept secrets, this guide covers everything you need to know.

✔ Tailored Recommendations – Whether you're a history buff, a food enthusiast, or an adventure seeker, you'll find recommendations to suit your travel style.

✔ Insider Tips – Avoid common tourist mistakes, uncover hidden gems, and get the best advice on where to eat, when to visit, and how to save money.

✔ Step-by-Step Itineraries – Whether you're visiting for a weekend or a week, this guide includes carefully curated itineraries to maximize your time.

✔ Cultural & Practical Information – Learn how to navigate Nice's public transport, understand local customs, and blend in seamlessly with the Niçois way of life.

Your Journey Starts Here

This guide is more than just a collection of travel tips—it's your passport to an unforgettable Nice experience. Whether you dream of strolling through the Old Town, savoring fresh seafood by the sea, or watching the sunset from Castle Hill, you'll find everything you need right here to craft the perfect trip.

So, as you turn the page, get ready to immerse yourself in the beauty, culture, and irresistible charm of Nice in 2025. Your adventure starts now!

ESSENTIAL TRAVEL INFORMATION

When planning a trip to Nice in 2025, being well-prepared can make all the difference between a smooth, stress-free experience and unexpected hurdles. From visa rules and budgeting tips to knowing the best time to visit, this section equips you with everything you need to navigate Nice like a pro.

Entry & Visa Requirements for 2025

Before packing your bags, it's crucial to check the latest entry requirements for France, as visa policies and regulations may change from year to year.

Visa Requirements

European Union (EU), European Economic Area (EEA), and Swiss Citizens

If you're traveling from an EU/EEA country or Switzerland, you do not need a visa to visit France. A valid passport or national ID card is sufficient.

United States, Canada, Australia, New Zealand, UK & Other Visa-Exempt Countries

Travelers from these countries can stay in France visa-free for up to 90 days within a 180-day period for tourism purposes. However, starting in mid-2025, visitors from these nations will need to complete an ETIAS (European Travel Information and Authorization System) application before departure. ETIAS is a simple online travel authorization that ensures travelers meet entry requirements.

Countries Requiring a Schengen Visa

If your country is not visa-exempt, you'll need to apply for a Schengen Visa before traveling to Nice. This visa allows stays of up to 90 days within a 180-day period and grants access to all Schengen Zone countries.

ETIAS for Visa-Exempt Travelers (Coming Mid-2025)

The ETIAS system is expected to be mandatory by mid-2025 for travelers from visa-exempt countries, including the USA, Canada, UK, and Australia. Here's what you need to know:

✔ Apply Online – The process is digital, with approval typically granted within minutes to hours.

✔ Fee – Expect a small processing fee (around €7 per adult, free for minors under 18).

✔ Validity – ETIAS approvals last for three years or until your passport expires.

✔ Requirement – You must have an ETIAS approval before boarding your flight.

Always double-check visa and entry requirements via France's official visa website or your nearest French consulate or embassy to ensure compliance with the latest rules.

Currency, Budgeting & Payment Tips (Including Hidden Costs)

Understanding how to handle money in Nice will save you from unnecessary stress, hidden costs, and potential overspending.

Currency in Nice

✔ Euro (€) is the official currency – Bills come in denominations of €5, €10, €20, €50, €100, €200, and €500, while coins range from 1 cent to €2.

✔ Card payments are widely accepted, especially Visa & Mastercard. However, carrying some cash is advisable for small markets, bakeries, and local vendors.

Budgeting for Nice in 2025

Nice can be as affordable or as luxurious as you want it to be. Here's a rough daily budget breakdown:

Budget Traveler (€50-€100 per day)

Hostels or budget hotels (€30-€60 per night)

Street food or bakeries (€5-€10 per meal)

Public transport (€1.70 per ride or €10 for a day pass)

Free attractions (beach, Old Town, Castle Hill)

Mid-Range Traveler (€100-€250 per day)

Boutique hotels or Airbnbs (€80-€150 per night)

Restaurant dining (€15-€30 per meal)

Entry fees to museums & activities (€10-€20 each)

Occasional taxi rides (€15-€25 per trip)

Luxury Traveler (€250+ per day)

Luxury hotels (€250-€1000 per night)

Fine dining (€50+ per meal)

Private tours, yacht rentals, and exclusive experiences

Hidden Costs to Watch Out For

☐ Tourist Tax – Hotels and Airbnbs charge a per-night tourist tax (€1-€4 per person per night).

☐ Restaurant Service Charge – A 10-15% service charge is included in most bills. Additional tipping is optional.

☐ ATM Fees – Some ATMs charge €3-€6 per withdrawal for foreign cards. Use bank-affiliated ATMs for better rates.

☐ Beach Rentals – Many private beaches charge for sunbeds (€20-€50 per day). Public beaches are free but pebbly—bring water shoes!

☐ Baggage Fees on Low-Cost Flights – Budget airlines charge extra for luggage, so check your baggage allowance before flying.

Best Time to Visit Nice (Weather, Crowds & Seasonal Highlights)

Nice is a year-round destination, but when you visit depends on what you're looking for—great weather, fewer crowds, or exciting events.

Spring (March – May) – Ideal for Sightseeing

Mild temperatures (12-20°C / 54-68°F)

Fewer crowds, perfect for exploring Old Town & coastal walks

Beautiful flower blooms and scenic countryside day trips

Summer (June – August) – Best for Beaches & Festivals

Hot & sunny (22-30°C / 72-86°F)

Peak beach season, buzzing nightlife

Major events like Nice Jazz Festival (July) and Bastille Day celebrations (July 14)

Very crowded & expensive—book accommodations months in advance!

Autumn (September – November) – Perfect Balance

Pleasant temperatures (15-25°C / 59-77°F)

Fewer tourists, ideal for wine country & cultural experiences

Stunning sunsets & warm Mediterranean waters until mid-October

Winter (December – February) – Off-Season Escape

Cool but comfortable (6-15°C / 43-59°F)

Nice Carnival (February) – One of Europe's best winter festivals

Lower prices & fewer crowds—great for budget travelers!

✔ Best for Beaches & Energy → Summer

✔ Best for Sightseeing & Comfort → Spring & Autumn

✔ Best for Budget & Events → Winter

Language & Useful French Phrases for Tourists

While many locals speak English, learning a few basic French phrases will enhance your experience and show respect for the culture.

Essential French Phrases for Tourists

Greetings & Basics:

   Bonjour! (Hello, good morning)

   Bonsoir! (Good evening)

   Merci! (Thank you)

   S'il vous plaît (Please)

   Excusez-moi (Excuse me)

Asking for Directions:

   Où est la plage? (Where is the beach?)

   Comment aller à la vieille ville? (How do I get to Old Town?)

   Où sont les toilettes? (Where are the restrooms?)

At Restaurants & Cafés:

Un menu, s'il vous plaît. (A menu, please.)

Je voudrais… (I would like…)

L'addition, s'il vous plaît. (The bill, please.)

Shopping & Payments:

Combien ça coûte? (How much does it cost?)

Acceptez-vous la carte de crédit? (Do you accept credit cards?)

✔ Tip: A friendly 'Bonjour' before asking for help goes a long way!

By preparing with these essential details, you'll navigate Nice with ease, avoid common pitfalls, and have a truly unforgettable experience in 2025.

3

GETTING TO NICE

Getting to Nice, France, is easier than ever, thanks to its well-connected airport, efficient train network, scenic roadways, and cruise-friendly port. Whether you're flying in from abroad, arriving by train from another European city, or cruising along the Mediterranean, this section ensures you arrive prepared, informed, and stress-free.

Arriving by Air: Nice Côte d'Azur Airport Guide

Nice Côte d'Azur Airport (NCE) is France's third-busiest airport, after Paris' Charles de Gaulle and Orly airports. Serving as the main international gateway to the French Riviera, it welcomes millions of travelers each year and provides direct connections to over 100 destinations worldwide.

Quick Facts About Nice Côte d'Azur Airport (NCE)

✔ Location – Just 7 km (4 miles) west of Nice city center

✔ Terminals – Two terminals (T1 & T2), both handling international and domestic flights

✔ Airlines – Serves major carriers like Air France, British Airways, Lufthansa, Emirates, EasyJet, and Ryanair

✔ Flight Time from Major Cities:

London: 2 hours

Paris: 1 hour 30 minutes

New York: 8 hours (direct)

Dubai: 6 hours 30 minutes

Getting from the Airport to Nice City Center

Upon landing, you have several transportation options to get to downtown Nice quickly:

By Tram (Best Budget Option – €1.70)

Line 2 (Ligne 2): Runs every 8-10 minutes, connecting both airport terminals to the city center.

Travel time: Around 20-25 minutes to Place Masséna (main square).

Cost: Only €1.70 for a single ticket or €10 for a day pass.

Tickets: Available at vending machines at the tram stop.

By Taxi (Most Convenient – €32 Fixed Fare)

Official airport taxis charge a fixed rate of €32 to anywhere in central Nice.

Travel time: Around 15-20 minutes (longer during rush hours).

Beware of scams – Always take a taxi from the official airport taxi stand.

Private Transfers (Luxury & Hassle-Free – €40-€60)

Services like Welcome Pickups, Uber, and private chauffeurs offer direct transfers.

Great for groups, families, or travelers with extra luggage.

Airport Express Bus (Affordable Alternative – €6.50)

Bus 98 & 99: Connects the airport to major hotels and train stations.

Takes 30-40 minutes, making it slower than the tram.

Pro Tip: If you're staying in the Old Town (Vieux Nice), taking the tram is your best bet, as taxis struggle with the narrow streets.

Getting to Nice by Train, Car, or Cruise Ship
Arriving in Nice by Train (Best for Comfort & Scenic Views)

Nice is well-connected to France and Europe's high-speed rail network, making train travel a comfortable, scenic, and eco-friendly way to reach the city.

✔ Main Station: Gare de Nice-Ville (Nice Central Station)

✔ TGV & Intercity Routes:

Paris → Nice (5h 30m via TGV)

Marseille → Nice (2h 30m)

Milan → Nice (5 hours)

Barcelona → Nice (8-10 hours via TGV & Intercity train)

✔ Regional TER Trains: Connect Nice to Monaco (20 min), Cannes (35 min), and Antibes (25 min).

✔ Train Tickets & Booking: Use SNCF Connect, Trainline, or Rail Europe for advance bookings.

Pro Tip: Book TGV tickets 2-3 months in advance for the best prices!

Driving to Nice (Best for Road Trippers)

If you love coastal drives, spontaneous stops, and exploring the French Riviera at your own pace, renting a car is a great option.

✔ Best Route from Paris:

Via A6 & A8 Motorway (~9 hours, tolls apply)

Stop in Lyon, Avignon, and Aix-en-Provence for a scenic journey

✔ Best Route from Italy:

Milan → Genoa → Nice (4-5 hours) along the Mediterranean coastline

Cross the stunning Italian-French border at Menton

✔ Parking in Nice:

Old Town (Vieux Nice) is pedestrianized, so park in public garages like Parking Sulzer or Nice Étoile (€20-€30 per day).

Avoid on-street parking—it's limited and expensive!

Driving Tip: The Promenade des Anglais has strict speed limits (50 km/h), and radar cameras are common. Drive carefully!

Arriving in Nice by Cruise Ship

Nice is a popular Mediterranean cruise destination, with most ships docking at the Port of Villefranche-sur-Mer, a picturesque harbor 15 minutes from Nice.

✔ **Cruise Lines Serving Nice:**

Royal Caribbean, MSC, Celebrity Cruises, Norwegian, and Ponant

✔ **Tender Boats to Shore:** Most large cruise ships anchor offshore and transport passengers to the port via small tender boats.

How to Get to Nice from Villefranche-sur-Mer:

By Train – TER train (7 minutes, €2.50) from Villefranche to Nice

By Taxi – €25-€35 for a direct ride into Nice

On Foot – A scenic coastal walk (~1 hour) if you're feeling adventurous!

Pro Tip: If you have limited time in port, book a private tour or shore excursion for a hassle-free experience.

Eco-Friendly Travel to Nice (Train vs. Flight Comparisons)

With growing concerns about sustainability and reducing carbon footprints, many travelers are opting for trains over flights when visiting Nice.

Train vs. Flight: Which is More Sustainable?

Route	Train CO$_2$ Emissions	Flight CO$_2$ Emissions	Eco-Friendly Option?
Paris → Nice	2.5 kg per passenger	92 kg per passenger	☐ Train
Milan → Nice	3 kg per passenger	60 kg per passenger	☐ Train
London → Nice	4 kg per passenger	130 kg per passenger	☐ Train
Barcelona → Nice	6 kg per passenger	75 kg per passenger	☐ Train

Why Choose the Train Over a Flight?

✔ Lower carbon footprint – Trains emit up to 90% less CO$_2$ than planes.

✔ No airport hassles – Skip security checks, baggage fees, and delays.

✔ Scenic experience – Enjoy gorgeous views of the French Riviera and countryside.

✔ Comfort & space – More legroom, free Wi-Fi, and no turbulence!

Best Eco-Friendly Routes to Nice:

Paris → Nice TGV – Takes 5h 30m, but saves a ton of emissions compared to a flight.

Milan → Nice Train – A 5-hour scenic ride along the Mediterranean coastline.

Eco-Travel Tip: If you must fly, choose direct flights to minimize emissions and fly with airlines using sustainable aviation fuel (SAF).

Final Thoughts

Whether you fly, take the train, drive, or cruise into Nice, each option has its own advantages. By choosing the right transportation method for your budget, schedule, and sustainability goals, you'll set the stage for an amazing journey to the heart of the French Riviera!

4

Getting Around Nice

Nice is a compact, pedestrian-friendly city with an efficient public transportation system, scenic walking routes, and a growing network of bike lanes. Whether you're taking the modern trams, hopping on a bus, cycling along the famous Promenade des Anglais, or using taxis and rideshares, getting around the city is convenient and accessible. This guide will help you navigate Nice effortlessly, ensuring you make the most of your time in this stunning French Riviera destination.

Public Transportation: Trams, Buses & Ticketing

Nice boasts a well-connected public transport system, primarily operated by Lignes d'Azur, the city's official transport network. Trams and buses cover almost every part of the city and nearby attractions, making them an affordable and reliable way to explore.

Trams: The Backbone of Public Transport in Nice

Nice's tram network is one of the fastest, cleanest, and most efficient ways to get around. The trams are frequent, modern, and eco-friendly, running every few minutes.

✔ **3 Tram Lines connect major neighborhoods, tourist spots, and transport hubs:**

Line 1: Serves central Nice, running from Henri Sappia to Hôpital Pasteur (great for Old Town, Place Masséna, and shopping areas).

Line 2: Connects Nice Côte d'Azur Airport to the city center and Port Lympia (ideal for travelers arriving by air).

Line 3: Extends Line 2 to the Allianz Riviera Stadium and western districts.

Tram Highlights:

✔ Frequent service – Runs every 3-5 minutes during peak hours.

✔ Affordable fares – A single ticket costs €1.70, and a day pass is €5.

✔ Late-night service – Runs until midnight.

✔ Eco-friendly – Fully electric, reducing carbon emissions in Nice.

Pro Tip: Buy a 10-trip card (€10) if you plan to use the tram frequently—it's cheaper than buying single tickets.

Buses: Covering Every Corner of Nice

While trams handle most of the heavy lifting in central Nice, buses are essential for reaching hilltop areas, beaches, and nearby towns like Eze, Villefranche-sur-Mer, and Monaco.

✔ **Key Bus Routes for Tourists:**

Bus 100: Runs along the coast to Monaco & Menton, offering breathtaking sea views (€2.50).

Bus 82 & 112: Go to Eze Village, a medieval hilltop town with stunning views.

Bus 98 & 99: Connect Nice Côte d'Azur Airport to the city center.

Bus Highlights:

✔ Frequent service in the city – Every 10-15 minutes during the day.

✔ Cheaper than taxis – Most rides cost €1.70.

✔ Ticketing is integrated – Use the same tickets for buses and trams.

Pro Tip: If you're heading to Monaco, the Bus 100 offers the same stunning sea views as the train, but for a fraction of the price.

Ticketing & How to Pay for Public Transport

Nice uses a unified ticketing system for trams and buses, making it easy to switch between both.

✔ Types of Tickets:

Single ticket (€1.70) – Valid for 74 minutes, allowing transfers between trams and buses.

Day pass (€5) – Unlimited travel for 24 hours.

Multi-trip card (€10 for 10 trips) – Best value for multiple rides.

7-day pass (€15) – Unlimited travel for a week.

✔ Where to Buy Tickets:

Ticket machines at tram stops (accepts cards & coins).

Tobacconists & convenience stores with the Lignes d'Azur sign.

Via the 'Lignes d'Azur' app (digital tickets available).

Pro Tip: Always validate your ticket before boarding! Ticket inspectors check frequently, and fines for non-validation start at €40.

Walking & Biking: The Best Way to Explore the City

Nice is one of the most walkable cities in France, with pedestrian-friendly streets, seaside promenades, and car-free zones in the Old Town. Walking is not just a mode of transportation—it's an experience in itself!

Walking in Nice: Explore at Your Own Pace

✔ **Top Walkable Areas:**

Old Town (Vieux Nice): Wander through charming alleys, colorful markets, and historic squares.

Promenade des Anglais: A 7 km seaside boulevard with breathtaking Mediterranean views.

Castle Hill (Colline du Château): Hike up for panoramic city views.

✔ **Why Walk?**

Most attractions are within 15-20 minutes of each other.

No need to worry about parking or traffic.

Walking lets you discover hidden gems (small cafés, local shops, and street performances).

Biking: Ride Along the Riviera

Nice is becoming more bike-friendly, with dedicated cycling lanes and a public bike-sharing system.

✔ **Where to Rent Bikes in Nice:**

Vélo Bleu (Public Bike Share) – €1 for 30 minutes or €5 per day.

Local Bike Rentals – Companies like Ebike Riviera Tour & Holland Bikes offer electric and standard bikes.

✔ **Best Cycling Routes:**

Promenade des Anglais – A scenic beachfront ride stretching to Cagnes-sur-Mer.

Nice to Villefranche-sur-Mer – A stunning coastal bike ride (great for a day trip).

Parc de la Colline du Château – Bike up for a workout with a view!

Pro Tip: Use electric bikes if you plan to explore Nice's hilly neighborhoods—they make uphill rides much easier!

Taxis, Rideshares & Car Rentals: What You Need to Know

Taxis in Nice (Expensive but Reliable)

✔ Fixed fares from the airport to the city center (€32).

✔ Taxi stands are available at major points (train station, airport, and Place Masséna).

✔ Call ahead or use apps like 'Taxi Riviera' to book.

Taxi Tips:

Taxis are expensive in Nice – Expect to pay €10-€15 for short rides.

Always ask for an estimated fare before getting in.

Avoid unofficial taxis—only use licensed cabs with a taxi sign.

Rideshares: Uber vs. Bolt

Uber and Bolt operate in Nice, often offering cheaper fares than taxis.

✔ Uber fares start at €7-€10 for short trips.

✔ Bolt is often 10-15% cheaper than Uber.

✔ Rideshare cars are cleaner and more modern than most taxis.

Downside: During peak tourist seasons, Uber prices surge, sometimes making taxis cheaper for short trips.

Renting a Car in Nice: Is It Worth It?

✔ Best for day trips to Monaco, Provence, and the French Riviera.

✔ Rental prices start at €35-€50 per day (cheaper if booked in advance).

✔ Parking is a nightmare in central Nice – avoid renting a car if you only plan to stay in the city.

When to Rent a Car?

If you're exploring beyond Nice (e.g., Provence, Verdon Gorge, or the Italian border).

If you're traveling in a group, splitting rental costs can be cheaper than train tickets.

Downside: Traffic in Nice can be heavy, and parking costs €20-€30 per day in public garages.

Final Thoughts

Whether you choose to walk, bike, take public transport, or use taxis, getting around Nice is easy and convenient. Plan based on your travel style and budget, and you'll enjoy every moment of your time in this breathtaking Riviera city!

5

WHERE TO STAY IN NICE

Finding the perfect place to stay in Nice is key to maximizing your experience in this dazzling French Riviera city. Whether you seek luxury with a sea view, a charming boutique hotel, an affordable yet comfortable stay, or an eco-friendly accommodation, Nice offers a wide range of options for every traveler.

This guide will help you decide where to stay based on your travel style and budget, covering the best neighborhoods, top hotels, and alternative lodging options.

Best Neighborhoods to Stay in Nice (Pros & Cons)

Nice is divided into distinct neighborhoods, each offering a unique experience. The right area depends on your budget, interests, and how you want to experience the city. Here's a breakdown of the top areas to stay in Nice, with their pros and cons.

1. Vieux Nice (Old Town) – Best for First-Time Visitors & Culture Lovers

Why Stay Here?

✔ Historic charm: Cobbled streets, colorful buildings, and lively markets.

✔ Close to attractions: Steps from Place Masséna, Cours Saleya, and Castle Hill.

✔ Great for foodies: Packed with authentic French cafés, wine bars, and bistros.

Downsides:

Can be crowded and noisy in peak seasons.

Fewer modern hotels—mostly small boutique stays and apartments.

Ideal for: Culture enthusiasts, first-time visitors, and travelers who love to explore on foot.

2. Promenade des Anglais – Best for Beach Lovers & Luxury Travelers

Why Stay Here?

✔ Spectacular sea views: Hotels directly face the Mediterranean.

✔ Luxury stays: Home to high-end hotels like Le Negresco & Hyatt Regency.

✔ Great for relaxation: Beachfront access, scenic walks, and sunset views.

Downsides:

Expensive—mostly luxury hotels and 4-5 star resorts.

Not as lively at night compared to Old Town.

Ideal for: Couples, honeymooners, and travelers who want uninterrupted sea views.

3. Carré d'Or – Best for Shopping & Upscale Dining

Why Stay Here?

✔ Central location: Near Avenue Jean Médecin (main shopping street).

✔ Stylish boutiques & fine dining: Upscale restaurants and designer stores.

✔ Close to both Old Town and the beach.

Downsides:

Hotels can be pricey.

Lacks the historic charm of Old Town.

Ideal for: Fashion lovers, business travelers, and those who want a modern, stylish atmosphere.

4. Liberation & Borriglione – Best for Budget Travelers & Local Vibes

Why Stay Here?

✔ Affordable hotels and rentals compared to central Nice.

✔ Great local markets & cafés without tourist crowds.

✔ Connected to the tram line for easy access to the city center.

Downsides:

Farther from the beach (20-30 min walk).

Less nightlife and entertainment options.

Ideal for: Budget-conscious travelers and those wanting a more authentic local experience.

5. Le Port – *Best for Nightlife & Young Travelers*

Why Stay Here?

✔ Trendy bars & restaurants: Great for nightlife and socializing.

✔ Unique boutique hotels & stylish apartments.

✔ Close to ferry terminals for trips to Corsica & nearby islands.

Downsides:

Can be noisy, especially on weekends.

Fewer hotel options—mostly Airbnbs & boutique stays.

Ideal for: Young travelers, solo adventurers, and partygoers.

6. Cimiez – *Best for a Quiet, Residential Stay*

Why Stay Here?

✔ Peaceful and green: Surrounded by parks, gardens, and museums.

✔ Great for families and long-term stays.

✔ Historic sites nearby (e.g., Roman ruins and the Matisse Museum).

Downsides:

Far from nightlife and the beach.

Limited public transport options.

Ideal for: Families, art lovers, and travelers who prefer a quiet retreat.

Top Hotels for Every Budget (Luxury, Mid-Range & Budget)

Whether you're looking for a lavish beachfront resort, a charming boutique stay, or an affordable hotel, Nice has fantastic accommodation options for every budget.

Luxury Hotels (€300+ per night)

✔ Hotel Negresco – Iconic 5-star hotel with Belle Époque elegance and a private beach.

✔ Hyatt Regency Nice Palais de la Méditerranée – Seafront luxury with a rooftop pool and spa.

✔ Boscolo Exedra Nice – An opulent Marble-filled 5-star stay with a wellness spa.

Best for: Honeymooners, luxury seekers, and those wanting a 5-star Riviera experience.

Mid-Range Hotels (€120-€300 per night)

✔ Hotel Le Grimaldi by HappyCulture – Charming 4-star boutique hotel in Carré d'Or.

✔ The Deck Hotel by HappyCulture – Modern and stylish, just a short walk from the beach.

✔ Hotel Suisse – Offers stunning sea views without the high price tag of luxury hotels.

Best for: Couples, families, and travelers looking for comfort without overspending.

Budget Hotels (€50-€120 per night)

✔ Ibis Styles Nice Centre Gare – Reliable budget-friendly option in a central location.

✔ Hôtel Ozz by HappyCulture – A chic and affordable boutique hotel with a youthful vibe.

✔ Hotel du Pin Nice Port – Affordable stay near Le Port, ideal for budget travelers.

Best for: Backpackers, solo travelers, and those wanting a low-cost but comfortable stay.

Alternative Stays: Airbnbs, Hostels & Eco-Friendly Lodging

If you prefer a more flexible or unique stay, consider Airbnbs, hostels, or sustainable hotels.

Airbnb & Vacation Rentals

✔ Great for families and longer stays.

✔ Options range from budget apartments to luxury penthouses.

✔ Some properties offer kitchenettes, helping save on food costs.

Pro Tip: Book well in advance—Airbnbs in Nice fill up quickly, especially in summer.

Hostels: Budget-Friendly Social Stays

✔ Hostel Meyerbeer Beach – Best for backpackers, just 2 minutes from the beach.

✔ Villa Saint Exupéry Beach Hostel – Features a bar, free breakfast, and dorm-style rooms.

✔ Antares Hostel – Affordable, clean, and right near the Nice-Ville train station.

Best for: Solo travelers and young adventurers wanting budget-friendly social stays.

Eco-Friendly Hotels & Sustainable Lodging

✔ Hotel Florence Nice – Certified eco-friendly, using solar energy and sustainable materials.

✔ Hi Hotel Eco Spa & Beach – A boutique hotel with organic dining and a green energy concept.

✔ Villa Rivoli – A charming eco-conscious boutique hotel in the city center.

Best for: Travelers seeking sustainable, responsible tourism.

Final Thoughts

Nice offers accommodation for every traveler, from luxury beachfront resorts to budget-friendly hostels and eco-conscious stays. By choosing the right neighborhood and hotel that fits your travel style, you'll ensure a comfortable and unforgettable experience on the French Riviera!

6

TOP ATTRACTIONS & LANDMARKS

Nice is a city that seamlessly blends history, culture, and natural beauty, making it one of the most exciting destinations on the French Riviera. Whether you want to stroll along a legendary promenade, wander through the colorful Old Town, marvel at panoramic views, or dive into world-class art and culture, Nice has something for everyone.

This section takes you on an in-depth journey through Nice's most iconic attractions, with insider tips and hidden gems to make your visit even more special.

The Promenade des Anglais: Nice's Most Famous Walk

The Promenade des Anglais is the heart and soul of Nice, stretching 7 kilometers (4.3 miles) along the Mediterranean coast. This palm-lined boulevard is one of Europe's most scenic waterfront walks, offering breathtaking sea views, stunning Belle Époque architecture, and a perfect setting for a leisurely stroll.

What to Expect on the Promenade

✔ Seafront Views – Gaze at the azure waters of the Baie des Anges as waves gently lap against the shore.

✔ Historic Landmarks – Spot iconic buildings like Le Negresco Hotel, Palais de la Méditerranée, and Villa Masséna.

✔ Beachside Bliss – Relax on the famous blue chairs or enjoy the private and public beaches along the promenade.

✔ Vibrant Atmosphere – Street performers, joggers, rollerbladers, and cyclists add to the lively energy.

Insider Tips

Best Time to Visit: Sunrise or sunset offers cooler temperatures and magical lighting.

Rent a Bike: Many visitors rent bicycles or electric scooters for a fun, breezy ride along the Promenade.

Look Out for Events: The Promenade hosts major events like the Nice Carnival (February) and Ironman France (June).

Location: Runs from Nice Airport to the Quai des États-Unis

Time Needed: 30 minutes to 2 hours (depending on how much you explore)

Exploring Vieux Nice (Old Town) – Must-See Spots & Hidden Gems

Vieux Nice is the historic and cultural heart of the city, a maze of narrow, winding streets, vibrant markets, and pastel-colored buildings. This is where you'll find local charm at its best, with bustling squares, baroque churches, and authentic eateries.

Must-See Spots in Vieux Nice

1. Cours Saleya Market – The Beating Heart of Old Town

Why Visit?

✔ Famous flower, fruit, and spice market with a lively atmosphere.

✔ Local vendors selling fresh produce, cheeses, and artisanal goods.

✔ Tuesdays: Transforms into a charming antique market.

Location: Cours Saleya

Time Needed: 30 minutes – 1 hour

2. Place Rossetti – A Picturesque Square

Why Visit?

✔ Home to Cathédrale Sainte-Réparate, a stunning baroque church with an ornate façade.

✔ Famous for Fenocchio's Gelateria, offering 100+ flavors of ice cream & sorbet.

✔ Beautiful fountain and lively cafés, perfect for people-watching.

Location: Place Rossetti

Time Needed: 20 – 40 minutes

3. Palais Lascaris – A Hidden Architectural Gem

Why Visit?

✔ A 17th-century aristocratic palace showcasing lavish baroque interiors.

✔ Houses one of France's largest collections of historic musical instruments.

✔ Often overlooked, making it a quiet, immersive cultural experience.

Location: 15 Rue Droite

Time Needed: 30 – 45 minutes

Insider Tips for Old Town

Best Time to Explore: Mornings (fewer crowds and cooler temperatures).

Wear Comfortable Shoes: The cobbled streets can be tricky to walk on.

Try Local Specialties: Taste socca (chickpea pancake) and pissaladière (onion tart) from a local food stall.

Castle Hill (Colline du Château) – Views, History & Secret Corners

Castle Hill is one of the most breathtaking viewpoints in Nice, offering panoramic vistas of the coastline, Old Town, and the Port of Nice. Once home to a medieval fortress, today it's a lush park with waterfalls, ruins, and scenic walking paths.

What to See on Castle Hill

1. Panoramic Lookout Points

Why Visit?

✔ The best photo spot in Nice with uninterrupted views of the Baie des Anges.

✔ Sunset views are particularly magical.

✔ Several hidden paths lead to quieter scenic spots.

2. Cascade du Château (Castle Hill Waterfall)

Why Visit?

✔ Artificial waterfall built in the 19th century, creating a serene, refreshing stop.

✔ A picturesque photo spot with a calming sound of cascading water.

✔ Perfect for a quick break after the uphill climb.

3. Ruins of the Old Castle & Cemeteries

Why Visit?

✔ Explore the remaining ruins of Nice's medieval castle.

✔ Visit the cemeteries at the top, where ornate tombs and sculptures tell fascinating stories.

Insider Tips for Castle Hill

How to Get There: Take the elevator from Quai des États-Unis or walk up the stairs from Old Town.

Best Time to Visit: Late afternoon for cooler weather and golden-hour views.

Bring Water & Snacks: There are limited food options at the top.

Location: East of Old Town

Time Needed: 1 – 2 hours

Nice's Best Museums & Cultural Experiences

Nice is home to world-class museums and cultural treasures, celebrating everything from modern art to ancient history.

Must-Visit Museums

1. Musée Matisse

Why Visit?

✔ Showcases Henri Matisse's masterpieces, housed in a 17th-century Genoese villa.

✔ Includes paintings, sculptures, and personal objects from Matisse's life in Nice.

✔ Surrounded by Cimiez Gardens, perfect for a post-museum stroll.

Location: 164 Avenue des Arènes de Cimiez

Time Needed: 1 hour

2. Musée Marc Chagall

Why Visit?

✔ Dedicated to the spiritual and poetic works of Marc Chagall.

✔ Features stunning stained-glass windows and biblical-themed paintings.

✔ One of Nice's most unique art museums.

Location: Avenue Docteur Ménard

Time Needed: 1 – 1.5 hours

3. Musée d'Art Moderne et d'Art Contemporain (MAMAC)

☐ Why Visit?

✔ Showcases modern and contemporary art, including Pop Art and New Realism.

✔ Houses works from Andy Warhol, Yves Klein, and Niki de Saint Phalle.

✔ Offers rooftop views of Nice from the museum's terrace.

Location: Place Yves Klein

Time Needed: 1 – 1.5 hours

Final Thoughts

Nice is a city filled with history, breathtaking views, and artistic treasures. Whether you're wandering the Old Town, climbing Castle Hill, exploring museums, or strolling the Promenade des Anglais, each attraction adds a unique layer to your experience on the French Riviera.

7

NICE BEYOND THE TOURIST SPOTS

While Nice is famous for its sun-drenched Promenade des Anglais, charming Old Town, and stunning seaside views, the city has a more intimate, local side that many visitors never get to experience. Beyond the tourist-packed attractions, you'll find hidden markets, secret alleys, tucked-away cafés, and authentic neighborhoods where locals live, work, and play.

If you're looking to go beyond the usual tourist experience and immerse yourself in the real Nice, this section will show you where to find the city's best-kept secrets, lesser-known neighborhoods, and local hangouts.

Local Markets, Secret Alleys & Hidden Cafés

One of the best ways to discover the soul of Nice is by exploring its local markets, quiet alleyways, and charming cafés tucked away from the main tourist routes.

Marché de la Libération – A True Local Market

Location: Avenue Malausséna, near the Libération tram stop

Best Time to Visit: Morning (7 AM – 1 PM, except Mondays)

While Cours Saleya Market in Old Town is famous among visitors, the Marché de la Libération is where locals actually do their shopping. This bustling market is packed with:

✔ Fresh fruits and vegetables from local farmers.

✔ Cheese and charcuterie stalls with authentic regional flavors.

✔ Fishmongers selling the freshest Mediterranean seafood.

✔ Bakeries with warm baguettes, buttery croissants, and traditional Nice pastries.

Insider Tip: Stop by Lou Pantail, a small bakery near the market, for a slice of pissaladière (onion tart) or a freshly baked fougasse (herbed bread).

The Secret Alleys of Old Town (Vieux Nice)

Vieux Nice is full of winding alleys and hidden corners that many tourists overlook. While exploring, look out for:

✔ Rue du Malonat – A tiny, winding alleyway with an old-world charm, leading up towards Castle Hill.

✔ Rue Droite – Home to the stunning Palais Lascaris, but also filled with small artist studios and vintage shops.

✔ Rue de la Préfecture – A quieter alternative to the crowded Cours Saleya, with independent boutiques and authentic bistros.

Insider Tip: As you explore, look up! Many buildings have colorful shutters, hidden balconies, and tiny details that reveal centuries of history.

Hidden Cafés & Local Hangouts

Forget the overpriced tourist cafés and head to these hidden gems where locals gather for coffee, pastries, and relaxed conversation.

1. Café de la Place (Place Garibaldi)

✔ A classic Niçois café with an old-world charm.

✔ Perfect for people-watching in the beautiful Garibaldi Square.

✔ Try the café noisette (espresso with a dash of milk) and soak in the local atmosphere.

2. Marinette (Tucked Away Near Port Lympia)

✔ A cozy, stylish café with homemade pastries and fresh brunch options.

✔ Try the homemade granola, fresh juices, or a creamy cappuccino.

✔ Popular among locals but still a well-kept secret.

3. Café Marché (A Hidden Gem in Old Town)

✔ A tiny café with farm-to-table food and a laid-back vibe.

✔ Great for organic coffee, fresh salads, and a quiet escape from tourist crowds.

Exploring Nice's Lesser-Known Neighborhoods

Most tourists stick to the Old Town and Promenade des Anglais, but Nice is a multi-layered city with unique districts that each offer something different. If you want to explore Nice like a true local, these lesser-known neighborhoods should be on your list.

1. Libération – The True Local Experience

Location: North of Avenue Jean Médecin, accessible by tram

✔ Why Visit?

A vibrant, untouristy district where you'll find locals shopping, eating, and socializing.

Home to Marché de la Libération, one of the best fresh markets in the city.

Surrounded by beautiful Belle Époque buildings and leafy streets.

Don't Miss: A visit to Bistrot du Fromager, a hidden wine bar specializing in local cheese and wine pairings.

2. Cimiez – The Elegant & Historic Side of Nice

Location: Hills above Nice, a short bus ride from the city center

✔ Why Visit?

A quiet, historic neighborhood known for its Roman ruins and stunning mansions.

Home to the Musée Matisse and the Franciscan Monastery & Gardens.

A peaceful alternative to the bustling city center.

Insider Tip: Pack a picnic and relax in the gardens of the Franciscan Monastery—one of Nice's most serene spots with a panoramic view.

3. Le Port – A Trendy, Up-and-Coming District

Location: Around Port Lympia, east of Old Town

✔ Why Visit?

Once a quiet dockside area, now transformed into a trendy hotspot.

Filled with bohemian cafés, stylish boutiques, and quirky wine bars.

Less crowded than Old Town but full of character.

Don't Miss: A visit to Deli Bo, a local favorite café with excellent pastries and organic brunch options.

How to Experience the City Like a Local

Want to blend in with Niçois life? Here's how:

1. Shop at Local Boulangeries Instead of Tourist Bakeries

Skip the commercial cafés and get your croissants and baguettes from a neighborhood boulangerie. Some favorites include:

✔ Boulangerie Jeannot – Famous for its pain bagnat (Niçois tuna sandwich).

✔ Pâtisserie Lac – One of the best spots for handcrafted chocolates and pastries.

2. Have an Apéro Like a Local

In Nice, the early evening ritual of "l'apéro" (pre-dinner drinks and snacks) is an essential part of life. Instead of heading to touristy restaurants, try:

✔ Les Distilleries Idéales – A classic Niçois bar serving pastis, local wines, and charcuterie boards.

✔ La Part des Anges – A small wine bar with a fantastic selection of organic and natural wines.

3. Visit the Secret Local Beaches

Most tourists flock to the busy Plage Beau Rivage, but locals prefer:

✔ Plage de la Réserve – A tiny, hidden beach near Port Lympia with crystal-clear water.

✔ Plage Coco Beach – A secluded rocky cove with stunning Mediterranean views.

Insider Tip: Bring water shoes—the beaches in Nice are pebbly, not sandy!

Final Thoughts

Nice isn't just about its famous landmarks and seafront beauty—it's a city with layers of history, local culture, and hidden treasures waiting to be explored. By stepping off the beaten path and embracing local markets, quiet alleyways, charming cafés, and unique neighborhoods, you'll discover a side of Nice that most tourists never see.

Whether you're sipping coffee in a tucked-away café, wandering through secret streets, or chatting with locals at a hidden wine bar, these experiences will turn your trip into something truly special—a journey through the real heart of Nice.

8

BEACHES & COASTAL EXPERIENCES

Nice, set along the stunning Baie des Anges (Bay of Angels), boasts a glittering Mediterranean coastline that is both breathtaking and diverse. Whether you're looking for a laid-back sunbathing experience, thrilling watersports, or luxurious beach clubs with gourmet dining, Nice has something for everyone.

However, beach culture in Nice is unique, and first-time visitors should know what to expect before heading to the shore. Unlike the sandy beaches of other Mediterranean destinations, Nice's beaches are mostly pebbled (called galets), making them distinct but sometimes challenging for sunbathers.

This guide will help you navigate public vs. private beaches, the best swimming spots, top beaches for relaxation, and how to enjoy dining by the water at some of the city's most exclusive beach clubs.

Public vs. Private Beaches: What to Expect

Public Beaches: Free but Basic

✔ Free to access—no entrance fee.

✔ Bring your own towel, umbrella, and beach mat (pebbles can be uncomfortable).

✔ Some have basic showers and public restrooms nearby.

✔ Generally more crowded, especially in summer.

✔ No sunbeds or waiter service.

Nice has several public beaches along the Promenade des Anglais. Some of the most popular ones include:

Plage du Centenaire – A central, well-maintained public beach with easy access.

Plage de Carras – The only dog-friendly beach in Nice.

Plage des Ponchettes – A classic public beach near Old Town, great for a quick dip.

Insider Tip: Bring water shoes, as the pebbles can be tough on your feet!

Private Beaches: Comfort & Luxury

✔ Paid entrance (between €20-€50 for a sunbed).

✔ Lounge chairs, umbrellas, and waiter service for food & drinks.

✔ Access to clean, private restrooms & showers.

✔ Some offer beachside massages, DJs, and cocktail bars.

Most private beaches are located along the Promenade des Anglais, and each has its unique atmosphere, from chic and trendy to family-friendly.

Popular private beaches in Nice include:

Plage Beau Rivage – Stylish, with an excellent restaurant and a lively cocktail scene.

Castel Plage – A stunning setting beneath Castle Hill, perfect for a luxurious beach day.

Ruhl Plage – One of the oldest beach clubs, offering classic Riviera charm.

Insider Tip: Many private beaches offer discounts if you book a full-day pass instead of just a half-day rental.

The Best Beaches for Swimming, Relaxing & Watersports

Best Beaches for Swimming

If you're looking for calm waters and easy access to the sea, these beaches are your best bet:

✔ Plage du Centenaire – Clear waters and gentle waves, ideal for casual swimming.

✔ Plage de la Réserve – A hidden local gem with natural rock formations, perfect for a refreshing dip.

✔ Plage Coco Beach – A scenic rocky cove offering deep waters for strong swimmers.

Insider Tip: The further east you go, the cleaner and calmer the water tends to be!

Best Beaches for Relaxing & Sunbathing

Looking for a tranquil spot to lounge? Try:

✔ Castel Plage – Luxurious setting with comfortable sunbeds.

✔ Plage Opéra – Offers both public and private areas, with a quieter atmosphere.

✔ Plage Mala (Cap d'Ail) – A short trip from Nice, this secluded cove is worth the journey.

Insider Tip: Arrive early in the morning or late afternoon to avoid peak crowds, especially in summer.

Best Beaches for Watersports & Adventure

For thrill-seekers, Nice has plenty of exciting water activities:

✔ Plage de Carras – The best place for jet skiing and parasailing.

✔ Plage des Marinieres (Villefranche-sur-Mer) – A sandy beach just outside Nice, great for paddleboarding and kayaking.

✔ Blue Beach – Offers a range of activities, including wakeboarding and flyboarding.

Insider Tip: For a unique experience, try a stand-up paddleboard (SUP) session at sunset—the Mediterranean at dusk is magical!

Beach Clubs, Sunbeds & Dining by the Water

For those looking to pair their beach day with gourmet food, cocktails, and a stylish atmosphere, Nice's beach clubs provide the ultimate Riviera experience.

Best Beach Clubs for Drinks & Cocktails

✔ Beau Rivage Beach – Trendy atmosphere, signature cocktails, and chic sunset vibes.

✔ Castel Plage – A sophisticated setting under Castle Hill, perfect for rosé by the sea.

✔ Le Galet – A relaxed yet stylish spot, great for a laid-back drink with ocean views.

Best Beachfront Restaurants

✔ Blue Beach Restaurant – Offers a delicious seafood menu, right on the beach.

✔ Le Plongeoir – A spectacular restaurant built on a rock above the sea, serving Mediterranean cuisine.

✔ Le Galet – Known for fresh pasta, grilled fish, and Riviera-style ambiance.

Insider Tip: Reservations are a must during peak summer months!

Renting Sunbeds & VIP Beach Experiences

If you want to spend the whole day lounging in comfort, consider renting a VIP sunbed.

✔ Cost: Expect to pay €20-€50 for a sunbed with service.

✔ Included: Umbrella, towel, and access to private showers.

Best VIP sunbed experiences:

✔ Ruhl Plage – Offers a classic Riviera feel with top-notch service.

✔ Opéra Plage – A stylish setting with a laid-back, intimate atmosphere.

✔ Castel Plage – Perfect for luxury and exclusivity.

Insider Tip: Many beach clubs offer special sunset deals, where you can enjoy a lounge chair, cocktail, and tapas for a reduced evening rate.

Final Thoughts

Nice's beaches are as diverse as the city itself, offering something for every type of traveler. Whether you're looking for a free public beach, a high-end private beach club, or an adventurous day on the water, you'll find the perfect seaside experience along the French Riviera.

Key Takeaways:

✔ Public beaches = Free but basic (bring your own towel & water shoes).

✔ Private beaches = Paid but luxurious (sunbeds, food, and comfort).

✔ Best for swimming = Plage du Centenaire, Plage Coco Beach.

✔ Best for relaxation = Castel Plage, Plage Mala.

✔ Best for watersports = Plage de Carras, Villefranche-sur-Mer.

✔ Best beach clubs = Beau Rivage, Castel Plage, Blue Beach.

By choosing the right beach for your preferences, you can experience the Mediterranean exactly the way you want—whether it's a budget-friendly dip in the sea, a romantic sunset cocktail, or a VIP luxury retreat by the water.

OUTDOOR ADVENTURES & DAY TRIPS

Nice is more than just a glamorous seaside destination—it's also a gateway to some of the most breathtaking outdoor adventures and day trips in the French Riviera. Whether you prefer hiking through scenic trails, exploring charming hilltop villages, or taking a day trip to nearby coastal gems like Monaco, Cannes, and Antibes, there's no shortage of exciting experiences waiting beyond the city limits.

This section will guide you through the best hiking and walking trails, top day trips, and lesser-known excursions for those looking to experience the French Riviera beyond the usual tourist hotspots.

The Best Hiking & Walking Trails Near Nice

The diverse landscape around Nice offers stunning coastal paths, panoramic viewpoints, and charming countryside walks. Whether you're an experienced hiker or just looking for a scenic stroll, these trails provide an excellent way to explore the region's natural beauty.

1. Sentier du Littoral (Cap de Nice to Villefranche-sur-Mer)

Starting Point: Coco Beach, Nice

Distance: 5 km (3.1 miles)

Time: 1.5 - 2 hours

Difficulty: Easy to moderate

This spectacular coastal trail follows the cliffs between Nice and Villefranche-sur-Mer, offering unbeatable sea views. Along the way, you'll pass hidden coves, dramatic rock formations, and lush Mediterranean vegetation. It's an ideal choice for those who want a leisurely but rewarding walk with plenty of opportunities to stop for a swim in crystal-clear waters.

Insider Tip: End your hike in Villefranche-sur-Mer and enjoy lunch at a seaside café before taking a short train ride back to Nice.

2. Mont Boron Hike

Starting Point: Parc du Mont Boron, Nice

Distance: 4 km (2.5 miles)

Time: 1 - 1.5 hours

Difficulty: Moderate

For one of the best panoramic views of Nice, this hike through Mont Boron Park is a must. The route takes you through lush pine forests, past Fort du Mont Alban, and rewards hikers with stunning views of the Mediterranean, the Bay of Angels, and even Monaco on a clear day.

Insider Tip: Start early in the morning or late in the afternoon to avoid the heat and capture the best light for photos.

3. Hike to Èze Village

Starting Point: Nice or Èze-sur-Mer

Distance: 6 km (3.7 miles)

Time: 1.5 - 2 hours

Difficulty: Moderate to challenging

Also known as the Nietzsche Path, this steep but rewarding trail leads from the coastal town of Èze-sur-Mer up to the medieval village of Èze, perched dramatically on a cliffside. The views along the way are absolutely breathtaking, and once you reach Èze, you can explore the Jardin Exotique, narrow cobbled streets, and charming artisan shops.

Insider Tip: After your hike, visit the famous Fragonard Perfume Factory in Èze before taking a bus or train back to Nice.

Day Trips to Monaco, Cannes & Antibes

Nice is perfectly positioned for quick and easy day trips to some of the most iconic cities along the French Riviera. With frequent train connections, you can explore Monaco, Cannes, and Antibes in a single day—or take your time and focus on just one destination.

1. Monaco – Glitz, Glamour & Royal Heritage

Travel Time: 20 minutes by train

Why Visit?

✔ Visit the Monte Carlo Casino—one of the world's most famous casinos.

✔ Explore the Prince's Palace of Monaco and see the Changing of the Guard.

✔ Stroll through the exotic gardens and Port Hercule, lined with superyachts.

✔ Discover the fascinating Oceanographic Museum, built into a cliffside.

Insider Tip: If you're visiting in May, check if your trip coincides with the Monaco Grand Prix, one of the world's most prestigious Formula 1 races.

2. Cannes – Film Festival Glamour & Golden Beaches

Travel Time: 30 minutes by train

Why Visit?

✔ Walk the Boulevard de la Croisette, lined with luxury hotels and designer boutiques.

✔ Visit the Palais des Festivals, where the Cannes Film Festival takes place.

✔ Relax on the sandy beaches (a contrast to Nice's pebbled shores).

✔ Take a ferry to Île Sainte-Marguerite, home to the mysterious Man in the Iron Mask prison.

Insider Tip: For a more local experience, explore the Le Suquet district, Cannes' charming old town with panoramic views.

3. Antibes – Art, History & Seaside Charm

Travel Time: 20 minutes by train

Why Visit?

✔ Wander through Old Town Antibes, filled with quaint streets and local markets.

✔ Visit the Picasso Museum, housed in a stunning castle overlooking the sea.

✔ Relax at the plage de la Gravette, a small sandy beach near the port.

✔ Walk along the scenic Sentier du Littoral, a coastal path with jaw-dropping views.

Insider Tip: Don't miss the Marché Provençal, Antibes' vibrant covered market, for fresh local produce, cheese, and flowers.

Hidden Villages & Off-the-Beaten-Path Excursions

For those looking to escape the crowds and discover the hidden gems of the Riviera, here are some lesser-known but stunning destinations worth visiting.

1. Saint-Paul-de-Vence – The Artist's Village

Travel Time: 45 minutes by bus

Why Visit?

✔ One of the most beautiful medieval villages in France.

✔ Home to the famous Fondation Maeght (modern art museum).

✔ A haven for artists, with galleries and workshops around every corner.

✔ Stunning views of the Provençal countryside.

Insider Tip: Have lunch at the legendary La Colombe d'Or, where Picasso and Matisse once dined.

2. Peillon – A Cliffside Village Frozen in Time

Travel Time: 1 hour by car

Why Visit?

✔ A truly untouched medieval village, perched on a rocky outcrop.

✔ No cars—just stone streets, ancient houses, and breathtaking scenery.

✔ Perfect for a peaceful retreat away from the Riviera's bustling cities.

Insider Tip: Wear comfortable shoes, as the village has steep, cobbled pathways.

3. Gorges du Verdon – The Grand Canyon of France

Travel Time: 2 hours by car

Why Visit?

✔ Hike, kayak, or drive through one of Europe's most spectacular canyons.

✔ Stunning turquoise waters and dramatic cliffs.

✔ Great for outdoor enthusiasts and nature lovers.

Insider Tip: Rent a pedal boat or kayak to fully experience the breathtaking turquoise river.

Final Thoughts

Nice is perfectly situated for outdoor lovers and explorers, offering breathtaking hikes, easy day trips to world-famous cities, and charming hidden villages. Whether you want to hike along the coast, explore glamorous Monaco, or discover a medieval village frozen in time, the adventures surrounding Nice will make your trip unforgettable.

10

FOOD & WINE IN NICE

Nice is a paradise for food lovers, blending Mediterranean flavors with French culinary finesse. Nestled between Provence and Italy, the city's cuisine reflects its diverse heritage—featuring fresh seafood, sun-ripened vegetables, aromatic herbs, and world-class wines. From bustling food markets to Michelin-starred restaurants, Nice offers something for every taste and budget.

Traditional Niçoise Dishes You Must Try

Nice's culinary identity is distinct from mainstream French cuisine, relying on local produce, olive oil, seafood, and Provençal herbs. Here are some must-try dishes:

1. Salade Niçoise – The Iconic Dish

What it is: A fresh, protein-packed salad made with tomatoes, hard-boiled eggs, anchovies or tuna, olives, and green beans, drizzled with olive oil.

Where to try it: Chez Pipo or Le Safari (Cours Saleya Market)

2. Socca – The Ultimate Niçoise Street Food

What it is: A crispy-yet-creamy chickpea pancake, cooked in a wood-fired oven and served in thin slices.

Where to try it: Chez Thérésa (in the Cours Saleya market)

3. Pan Bagnat – The Niçoise Sandwich

What it is: A sandwich version of Salade Niçoise, stuffed inside a crusty round roll.

Where to try it: Lou Balico

4. Pissaladière – Niçoise Onion Tart

What it is: A pizza-like tart topped with caramelized onions, anchovies, and black olives.

Where to try it: René Socca

5. Ratatouille – The Classic Provençal Stew

What it is: A slow-cooked dish of eggplant, zucchini, bell peppers, and tomatoes, bursting with flavor.

Where to try it: Acchiardo

6. Daube Niçoise – Rich Beef Stew

What it is: A slow-cooked beef stew in red wine, tomatoes, onions, and Provençal herbs.

Where to try it: La Table Alziari

7. Tourte de Blettes – A Sweet Swiss Chard Pie

What it is: A unique Niçoise dessert made with Swiss chard, apples, pine nuts, and raisins, dusted with powdered sugar.

Where to try it: Pâtisserie Auer

Best Restaurants for Every Budget

Nice caters to all budgets, from affordable local bistros to luxurious fine dining spots.

Budget-Friendly (€-€€) – Great Taste, Low Cost

✔ Chez René Socca – Best for socca, pissaladière, and pan bagnat (€)

✔ La Cantine de Lulu – Cozy, family-run spot for Niçoise home cooking (€€)

✔ Lou Pilha Leva – Street food favorite serving Niçoise specialties (€)

Mid-Range (€€-€€€) – Authentic Local Cuisine

✔ Le Bistrot d'Antoine – A top-rated bistro for traditional Niçoise cuisine (€€€)

✔ La Merenda – Run by a former Michelin-star chef, offering classic Provençal dishes (€€)

✔ Oliviera – Perfect for olive oil-tasting with fresh Mediterranean dishes (€€)

Fine Dining (€€€€) – Michelin Stars & Riviera Elegance

✔ JAN ☐ – Michelin-starred South African-French fusion by Chef Jan Hendrik van der Westhuizen (€€€€)

✔ Le Chantecler ☐ ☐ – Inside the legendary Negresco Hotel, serving exquisite French cuisine (€€€€)

✔ Flaveur ☐ ☐ – Creative, modern French cuisine with Mediterranean influences (€€€€)

Wine, Cocktails & Riviera Drinks

The French Riviera is renowned for its wines and stylish bars. Whether you prefer a crisp glass of rosé, a handcrafted cocktail, or a taste of local spirits, Nice has plenty to offer.

Best Wine Bars & Wineries

✔ La Part des Anges – Cozy, organic wine bar with great charcuterie

✔ Cave Bianchi – Wine shop + tasting room, featuring local Provence wines

✔ Domaine de Toasc – A vineyard near Nice offering guided wine tastings

Best Cocktail & Rooftop Bars

✔ Le Plongeoir – Stunning over-the-water cocktail bar

✔ Le Bar du Negresco – Luxurious cocktail lounge inside the historic Negresco Hotel

✔ Movida – Trendy seafront bar with amazing sunset views

Riviera Spirits & Local Specialties

✔ Pastis – Classic anise-flavored aperitif

✔ Rosé Wine – The signature drink of the French Riviera

✔ Limoncello – A popular Italian-French citrus liqueur

Where to Find the Best Bakeries, Ice Cream & Coffee Shops

Nice is home to fantastic boulangeries, artisan coffee spots, and gelato shops.

Best Bakeries for Fresh Bread & Pastries

✔ Pâtisserie Auer – Famous for Tourte de Blettes & chocolates

✔ Boulangerie Jeannot – The best baguettes & croissants in town

✔ Maison Cangemi – Traditional French bakery with delicious pastries

Best Ice Cream & Gelato Shops

✔ Fenocchio – Over 90 flavors of ice cream & sorbet, including lavender & olive

✔ Arlequin Gelati – Authentic Italian gelato in Nice

Best Coffee Shops for a Morning Boost

✔ Café Marché – Specialty coffee + homemade pastries

✔ Malongo Café – One of the best espresso & cappuccino spots

✔ Brulerie des Cafés Indien – A historic coffee roastery in Old Nice

Special Diets: Vegetarian, Vegan & Gluten-Free Dining

Nice has embraced healthy eating trends, offering great options for vegetarians, vegans, and gluten-free travelers.

Best Vegetarian & Vegan Restaurants

✔ Koko Green – 100% vegan & organic cuisine

✔ Badaboom – Plant-based dishes + vegan desserts

✔ Paper Plane – A vegetarian brunch favorite

Best Gluten-Free Dining

✔ Le Speakeasy – Gluten-free galettes (savory crêpes)

✔ Gigi Tavola – Italian gluten-free pizza & pasta

Final Thoughts

Nice is one of France's top foodie destinations, combining Mediterranean flavors, fresh ingredients, and world-class wines. Whether you're indulging in a classic Niçoise dish, sipping a Riviera cocktail, or discovering a hidden local bakery, the culinary scene in Nice is sure to impress.

11

SHOPPING & SOUVENIRS IN NICE

Nice is a shopper's paradise, blending French elegance, Mediterranean charm, and Provençal tradition. Whether you're looking for designer fashion, artisan crafts, gourmet treats, or local souvenirs, the city offers a shopping experience that caters to all tastes and budgets. From luxury boutiques along Avenue Jean Médecin to bustling outdoor markets in Vieux Nice, here's a detailed guide to the best shopping experiences in Nice.

Where to Shop: Best Streets & Markets

Markets: The Heart of Local Shopping

For an authentic French shopping experience, explore Nice's lively outdoor markets. These are perfect for finding fresh produce, handmade goods, and traditional souvenirs.

1. Cours Saleya Market – Nice's Most Famous Market

✔ **Best for:** Local produce, flowers, and souvenirs

✔ **What to buy:** Lavender sachets, herbes de Provence, artisanal soaps, and regional wines

✔ **Open:** Tuesday–Sunday (morning until early afternoon)

Location: Vieux Nice (Old Town)

Tip: On Mondays, the market transforms into a flea market (Marché à la Brocante), great for antique hunting.

2. Liberation Market – Local's Favorite

✔ **Best for:** Fresh fruit, seafood, cheese, and regional specialties

✔ **What to buy:** Olive oils, truffle products, Provençal honey

✔ **Open:** Every morning except Monday

Location: Place du Général de Gaulle

Tip: Grab a freshly baked baguette and some local cheese for a picnic!

3. Nice Etoile Shopping Mall – Everything Under One Roof

✔ **Best for:** Fashion, beauty, electronics, and home décor

✔ **What to buy:** French and international brands like Zara, H&M, Sephora, and FNAC

✔ **Open:** Monday–Saturday, 10 AM – 7:30 PM

Location: Avenue Jean Médecin

Tip: Perfect for a rainy day shopping spree.

Unique Souvenirs & Local Crafts

If you want to take home authentic Niçoise gifts, look for these locally made specialties:

1. Provençal Herbs & Olive Oils

Nice is famous for its aromatic herbs and olive oil, used in traditional Mediterranean cooking.

Where to buy:

✔ Alziari Boutique – One of Nice's oldest olive oil producers

✔ Cours Saleya Market – Great for herbes de Provence & lavender

2. *Artisan Soaps & Perfumes*

Handmade savon de Marseille (Marseille soap) and locally produced perfumes make great gifts.

Where to buy:

✔ Fragonard Perfume Factory – One of France's most famous perfume houses

✔ La Maison du Savon de Marseille – Beautifully scented soap bars

3. *Candied Fruits & Sweets*

Nice is famous for its candied fruits, chocolates, and nougat.

Where to buy:

✔ Pâtisserie Auer – Traditional candied fruits & chocolates

✔ Confiserie Florian – Handmade Nougat & sweets

4. *Local Art & Handicrafts*

Nice has a vibrant arts scene, and you can find handmade ceramics, paintings, and jewelry.

Where to buy:

✔ Galerie Ferrero – Local contemporary art

✔ Marché des Antiquaires (Antique Market) – Vintage treasures

Luxury Shopping & Designer Boutiques

For those looking to splurge, Nice offers high-end boutiques and luxury shopping districts.

Avenue de Verdun – High-End Fashion

✔ Home to luxury brands like Louis Vuitton, Chanel, Dior, and Hermès

✔ Perfect for designer handbags, perfumes, and accessories

Galeries Lafayette – France's Iconic Department Store

✔ Offers a mix of high-end & mid-range fashion

✔ Great for French designer brands, cosmetics, and accessories

Location: Place Masséna

Carré d'Or – Nice's Fashionable District

✔ The most elegant shopping area in Nice

✔ Features luxury boutiques, jewelers, and haute couture designers

Location: Between Place Masséna and the Promenade des Anglais

Final Thoughts

Shopping in Nice is an unforgettable experience, whether you're hunting for luxury brands, artisan crafts, or gourmet souvenirs. From traditional markets to designer boutiques, the city offers something for every shopper.

Top Tip: Don't forget the French VAT refund! If you spend over €100.01 in a single store, you may be eligible for a tax refund on your purchases.

12

NICE'S NIGHTLIFE & ENTERTAINMENT

When the sun dips below the horizon and the Mediterranean sky transforms into a tapestry of deep blues and vibrant purples, Nice awakens with a pulse all its own. The city's nightlife is a dynamic blend of elegance, energy, and a laid-back Riviera charm—a playground for those who love to experience life in full color after dark.

Rooftop Bars, Beachfront Lounges & Jazz Clubs

Imagine stepping out onto a rooftop terrace where the panoramic vista of the twinkling Mediterranean meets the twinkling city lights below. Nice boasts a collection of rooftop bars that offer not only sumptuous cocktails but also an unrivaled atmosphere where every sip of your drink is accompanied by breathtaking views. Picture yourself at a chic bar perched atop a luxury hotel, the gentle sea breeze carrying whispers of the ocean, as you watch the sunset turn the sky into a masterpiece of oranges and pinks.

Down at the water's edge, beachfront lounges exude a relaxed sophistication. Here, the pace is slower, the vibe more intimate. You can settle into a plush sunbed, your feet almost touching the warm pebbles of the beach, while enjoying a signature cocktail and the sound of gentle waves. These lounges often blend the casual charm of a seaside retreat with the polished service of high-end hospitality—perfect for unwinding after a day of exploration.

For the music aficionados, Nice's jazz clubs are a treasure trove of soulful rhythms and intimate performances. In dimly lit, atmospheric venues tucked away in the winding streets of the Old Town, live jazz bands play tunes that resonate with both nostalgia and innovation. I've experienced nights where the smooth, sultry sounds of a saxophone seemed to encapsulate the very essence of the Riviera, turning an ordinary evening into a memorable celebration of art and life.

Casinos & Evening Shows

For those with a taste for a touch of glamour and a dash of high-stakes excitement, Nice offers a sophisticated array of casinos and evening shows. Step into a world where elegance meets adrenaline: luxurious casinos invite you to test your luck amid opulent interiors and attentive service. Here, the clinking of glasses, the soft hum of conversation, and the occasional cheer from a winning table create a captivating ambience that is both thrilling and refined.

Beyond the gaming floors, Nice's evening entertainment extends into theater, live music, and cabaret shows. Whether you're in the mood for a dazzling performance at an intimate venue or a grand production that recalls the golden age of European cabaret, you'll find options that promise to enchant. These shows often feature a blend of modern artistry with classic influences, ensuring that every performance is as unpredictable as it is captivating.

The Best Late-Night Experiences in Nice

As midnight approaches, Nice transforms yet again. The late-night scene here is a vibrant mix of energetic dance clubs, relaxed after-hours lounges, and even hidden speakeasies waiting to be discovered. After a sumptuous dinner and a few glasses of local rosé, the city offers myriad ways to continue your evening in style.

Stroll along the Promenade des Anglais, where the night air carries a subtle magic and the neon reflections on the water invite you to lose yourself in the moment. For those who crave the dance floor, several clubs pulse with energy until the early hours, each with its unique vibe—ranging from intimate, underground spots with eclectic music to sprawling, high-energy dance halls where world-class DJs set the beat.

If you prefer a quieter late-night experience, find a cozy bar tucked away in a narrow street or a hidden lounge where you can enjoy a final cocktail in peaceful elegance. Many locals know of secret spots that offer a relaxed atmosphere, perfect for reflective conversation or simply watching the world go by as Nice's vibrant nightlife slowly winds down.

In Summary:

Nice's nightlife and entertainment scene is a dynamic canvas painted with elegant rooftop retreats, relaxed beachfront vibes, soulful jazz sessions, thrilling casinos, and unforgettable late-night escapades. Whether you're sipping a signature cocktail high above the city, reveling in the excitement of a live show, or dancing until dawn, Nice invites you to experience the magic of the Riviera after dark—an experience that is as diverse and unforgettable as the city itself.

13

FESTIVALS & EVENTS IN 2025

In Nice, every season bursts with a kaleidoscope of festivals and events that transform the city into a living, breathing celebration of art, culture, and joie de vivre. In 2025, the French Riviera continues its tradition of hosting world-class events that cater to every interest—from the exuberant spectacle of the Nice Carnival to intimate local food fairs and international sporting events. Let's dive into what you can expect and how to make the most of these unforgettable experiences.

Nice Carnival: What to Expect & How to Experience It Best

Every winter, Nice comes alive with the magic and mischief of the Nice Carnival, one of the largest and most colorful festivals in Europe. This centuries-old tradition transforms the city into a fantastical realm where masks, costumes, and elaborate floats take center stage.

Imagine wandering through the narrow streets of Old Town as vibrant parades wind their way past you. The air is filled with contagious energy, music, and laughter as locals and visitors alike embrace the carnival spirit. The festivities feature an eclectic mix of traditional Niçois folklore, modern artistic expressions, and interactive street performances. In 2025, the carnival promises even more immersive experiences with themed parades, masked balls in historic venues, and art installations that blend past and present.

How to Experience It Best:

Plan Ahead: Book your accommodation early, as hotels fill up fast during carnival season.

Join the Parade: Don't just be a spectator—participate by donning a mask or costume. Many local workshops offer rentals and even classes on traditional Niçois mask-making.

Explore Hidden Corners: While the main parades are spectacular, some of the most memorable moments happen in the quiet, unexpected alleys where local groups perform impromptu dances and musical numbers.

Stay Safe: Keep an eye on your belongings, and embrace the local custom of sharing in the festivities with a spirit of camaraderie and fun.

For me, experiencing the Nice Carnival is like stepping into a living fairytale—where every street corner holds a secret performance and every smile hints at a story waiting to be discovered.

Music, Food & Art Festivals Throughout the Year

Beyond the carnival, Nice hosts a variety of festivals that celebrate its rich cultural tapestry. Whether you're a music aficionado, a culinary explorer, or an art lover, there's an event on the calendar to suit your passion.

Music Festivals:

The Nice Jazz Festival is a summer highlight, attracting renowned international artists and local talent alike. Set against the backdrop of the azure sea, this festival turns the city into a giant open-air concert, where smooth jazz rhythms blend seamlessly with the sounds of the Mediterranean. Additionally, La Fête de la Musique fills the streets with impromptu performances, transforming everyday public spaces into vibrant stages.

Food Festivals:

Foodies will delight in seasonal gastronomic events that celebrate Niçoise cuisine. From lively food markets that showcase the best of local produce to dedicated culinary fairs where top chefs demonstrate their skills, the region's food festivals offer hands-on workshops, tasting sessions, and even cooking classes that let you bring a piece of Nice's culinary heritage back home. Expect plenty of opportunities to savor delicacies like socca, pissaladière, and fresh seafood, all paired with a glass of crisp local wine.

Art Festivals:

Art and culture thrive in Nice through events like the Festival of Contemporary Art, where cutting-edge installations and avant-garde performances transform public spaces. Street art festivals paint the city with vibrant murals, and galleries host exhibitions that blend historical art with modern perspectives. These events are designed not only to display art but also to create interactive experiences where visitors can engage directly with the creative process.

How to Make the Most of These Festivals:

Stay Informed: Check local event calendars and social media for the latest updates, as many festivals feature last-minute pop-ups and secret shows.

Mix It Up: Don't stick to one genre—try attending a jazz night, a food tasting, and an art exhibit to get a full spectrum of what Nice has to offer.

Interact: Engage with local artists, chefs, and musicians. Their stories provide a deeper insight into the vibrant culture of Nice, enriching your experience beyond the surface-level spectacle.

Sporting Events & Cultural Celebrations

Nice isn't just about arts and food—it's also a hub for sports and cultural festivities that bring the community together in spirited celebration. In 2025, the city hosts a variety of events that cater to sports enthusiasts and those looking for dynamic cultural interactions.

Sporting Events:

Whether you're watching or participating, the sporting scene in Nice is invigorating. The Nice Half Marathon and the Mediterranean Triathlon draw athletes from around the world, offering routes that showcase the breathtaking scenery of the coastline and cityscape. For those who enjoy cycling, local races and charity rides offer a fun way to experience the region's natural beauty up close. Spectators can also catch local football matches or even sailing regattas along the harbor, each event radiating the competitive yet festive spirit of the Riviera.

Cultural Celebrations:

Throughout the year, various cultural events celebrate the diverse heritage of Nice. Fête de la Citron, although more associated with nearby Menton, spills over into Nice with citrus-themed parades and art installations that highlight the region's love for vibrant colors and fresh flavors. Traditional dances, folk music performances, and theatrical productions often take place in public squares and historic venues, inviting everyone to participate in centuries-old customs reimagined for modern audiences.

How to Embrace These Experiences:

Join a Local Tour: Many events offer guided tours or participatory sessions. Joining these can provide a deeper understanding of the cultural context behind the celebration.

Mix Sport with Leisure: If you're an active traveler, consider participating in one of the local races or triathlons, then unwind with a post-event gathering at a local café or wine bar.

Celebrate Diversity: Attend a mix of events—from the high-energy sporting competitions to the reflective cultural ceremonies—to appreciate the full spectrum of Nice's vibrant community life.

Final Thoughts:

In 2025, Nice's festivals and events are more than just dates on a calendar—they are immersive experiences that invite you to live, laugh, and celebrate like a true local. Whether you're marveling at the riot of colors and sounds during the Carnival, sampling exquisite flavors at a food festival, or cheering at a sporting event under the Riviera sun, each festival in Nice offers a doorway into the heart and soul of this enchanting city. Embrace the moments, engage with the locals, and let the vibrant celebrations of Nice leave an indelible mark on your journey.

14

NICE FOR EVERY TYPE OF TRAVELER

Nice isn't just a destination—it's a multifaceted experience that caters to every kind of traveler. Whether you're visiting with your family, seeking a romantic escape, journeying solo, or exploring on a budget, Nice unfolds its charm in diverse ways. Let's explore how this dazzling city on the French Riviera meets the needs and dreams of every traveler.

Family-Friendly Attractions & Activities

For families, Nice is a vibrant tapestry of fun, learning, and relaxation. Picture your children's eyes lighting up as you stroll along the Promenade des Anglais, where the shimmering Mediterranean and lively street performers create a magical backdrop. Families can spend afternoons building sandcastles on the pebbled shores or enjoying an impromptu picnic in one of the city's many green spaces.

One of the top family spots is Parc Phoenix, a botanical garden and zoo that offers interactive exhibits, lush tropical gardens, and a chance to see exotic animals up close. The park's playgrounds and themed gardens make it an ideal setting for kids to explore while adults relax under the Mediterranean sun.

In addition, **Old Town (Vieux Nice)** is a treasure trove of history and culture that appeals to curious minds. The narrow, winding streets are filled with vibrant markets, where children can marvel at the burst of colors from fresh flowers and local produce. Stop by the Cours Saleya Market for a sensory feast—here, the aroma of freshly baked goods and the chatter of local vendors add to the immersive experience.

For educational yet fun excursions, consider a visit to the Musée d'Art Moderne et d'Art Contemporain (MAMAC), where interactive exhibits make art accessible to even the youngest visitors. And when hunger strikes, family-friendly bistros and creperies offer hearty, comforting meals that cater to all palates.

In Nice, family travel is not just about sightseeing—it's about creating shared memories that are as warm and enduring as the Riviera sunshine.

Romantic Getaways & Honeymoon Ideas

Imagine a city where every sunset paints a new masterpiece, every narrow alley holds a secret, and every meal feels like a private celebration. That's Nice for couples seeking romance. With its timeless elegance and intimate settings, Nice is the perfect backdrop for love stories, whether you're on a honeymoon or planning a romantic getaway.

Begin your day with a leisurely breakfast at a quaint café in Vieux Nice, where the aroma of freshly baked croissants and rich espresso sets the tone for romance. A stroll along the Promenade des Anglais at sunrise offers a quiet, shared moment with the endless blue sea as your witness.

For a truly unforgettable experience, ascend Castle Hill (Colline du Château) at dusk. The panoramic views of the city, bathed in the golden hues of the setting sun, create a picture-perfect moment that seems almost tailor-made for romance. Enjoy a picnic on the hilltop, savoring local cheeses, fruits, and a chilled bottle of rosé, as you watch the world transform around you.

When it's time for dinner, indulge in a candlelit meal at one of Nice's gourmet restaurants. Many establishments offer intimate dining experiences, complete with terrace seating that overlooks the bustling streets or the tranquil sea. Whether you choose a high-end restaurant in the Carré d'Or district or a hidden gem in a quiet alley, the culinary delights of Nice are sure to impress.

For honeymooners, luxurious stays in boutique hotels with private terraces and spa services provide the ultimate pampering experience. In Nice, every detail—from the gentle sea breeze to the charming local traditions—invites you to slow down, savor the moment, and let love flourish.

Solo Travel & Social Spots

Traveling solo in Nice is like having a personal invitation to explore life at your own pace, and the city embraces every visitor with open arms. As a solo traveler, you'll find Nice exceptionally welcoming, with an array of social spots, guided tours, and community experiences designed to help you connect, explore, and truly immerse yourself in local life.

Start your day by joining one of the many free walking tours available in the city. These tours are not only an excellent way to learn about the rich history of Nice but also provide a fantastic opportunity to meet fellow travelers. Whether you're wandering through the charming lanes of Vieux Nice or exploring the modern art at MAMAC, you'll quickly discover that Nice has a friendly, unpretentious vibe that makes solo travel enjoyable and secure.

For those evenings when you crave social interaction, the city's lively cafés and bars come alive. In neighborhoods like Le Port and Carré d'Or, you'll find cozy, inviting spaces where locals and visitors mingle over drinks. Many solo travelers report that sharing a table at a bustling café or joining a communal dinner in a local bistro is a great way to forge new friendships and gain insider tips.

Art lovers and culture enthusiasts can also benefit from joining local events, such as gallery openings, music nights, or language exchange meet-ups. These events are a fantastic way to dive into the local scene, where the mix of modern creativity and traditional charm makes every encounter a learning experience.

Moreover, solo travelers on a budget will appreciate the abundance of public parks, museums with discounted entry days, and inexpensive public transportation options that make getting around Nice both economical and easy. In Nice, every street and square has a story to tell—and when you're exploring alone, every moment becomes an opportunity for personal discovery.

Budget Travel: How to Experience Nice for Less

Experiencing the French Riviera doesn't have to break the bank. Even on a tight budget, Nice offers a wealth of opportunities to enjoy its sun-soaked streets, cultural treasures, and culinary delights without compromising on quality.

Start with free or low-cost activities that showcase the city's natural beauty. The Promenade des Anglais is a prime example—this iconic seaside walkway is free to explore, offering endless views, public art installations, and a chance to watch the local life unfold. Enjoy a picnic with provisions from local markets, where fresh produce and artisanal goods are available at reasonable prices.

For sightseeing, take advantage of the numerous free museums and cultural sites. Many of Nice's attractions, such as its vibrant parks, historical squares, and even some art galleries, have no entrance fee or offer discounted rates on certain days of the week. Use the efficient public transportation system—the integrated tram and bus network—to hop from one attraction to another at minimal cost. A day pass or multi-trip card is not only economical but also allows you to explore the city without worrying about individual ticket prices.

Accommodations on a budget are plentiful in Nice. Opt for hostels, guesthouses, or budget hotels located in neighborhoods like Liberation or Le Port, where you can find comfortable stays at a fraction of the price of luxury accommodations. Consider booking an Airbnb or even a dorm room in a well-rated hostel to meet other travelers and share experiences.

Dining on a budget doesn't mean missing out on the flavors of Nice. Street food stalls, casual bistros, and local cafés offer hearty, authentic meals like socca, pissaladière, and pan bagnat at wallet-friendly prices. Food markets such as Cours Saleya provide not only a feast for the eyes but also a chance to pick up fresh ingredients for a self-catered meal if your accommodation offers a kitchen.

Moreover, plan your visit during the shoulder seasons—spring and autumn—when prices for accommodations and flights tend to be lower and the city is less crowded. Budget travel in Nice is all about being resourceful, planning ahead, and embracing the local way of life without the need for extravagant expenses.

In Summary:

Whether you're a family eager to create lasting memories, a couple seeking a romantic retreat, a solo adventurer in search of new connections, or a budget traveler determined to experience the best of the Riviera without overspending, Nice welcomes you with an array of tailored experiences. Each corner of this vibrant city holds a unique promise—of discovery, of connection, and of living life with passion and ease on the sun-drenched shores of the French Riviera.

15

SUSTAINABLE & RESPONSIBLE TRAVEL IN NICE

Traveling sustainably in Nice isn't just about reducing your carbon footprint—it's about embracing a philosophy that enriches your experience while supporting the local community and preserving the natural beauty of the French Riviera. In a city where history, culture, and nature intertwine, sustainable and responsible travel creates a deeper, more authentic connection with both the place and its people. Here's how you can explore Nice in an eco-friendly, ethical way that benefits you and the local community.

How to Travel Sustainably in Nice

Imagine strolling along sunlit cobblestone streets knowing that your journey is both enriching and gentle on the environment. In Nice, sustainable travel is woven into everyday life. One of the best ways to experience this is by choosing active and public transportation.

Walking & Biking:

Nice's compact layout makes it one of the most walkable cities in France. Meandering through the narrow alleys of Vieux Nice or along the famed Promenade des Anglais not only gives you a closer look at the city's soul but also keeps your environmental impact minimal. For longer distances, consider renting a bike or using the public bike-share system like Vélo Bleu. Electric bikes are a fantastic option if you want to tackle the city's gentle slopes with ease.

Public Transport:

The efficient network of trams and buses managed by Lignes d'Azur is a sustainable choice for navigating the city. A single ticket, valid for both buses and trams, opens up all corners of Nice while keeping emissions low. Many locals rely on these systems daily, and joining them is an excellent way to feel a part of the city's rhythm.

Eco-Friendly Tours:

When booking tours, look for operators who emphasize sustainability. Many local companies offer walking, cycling, or even segway tours that highlight eco-friendly practices and provide insightful commentary on Nice's green initiatives. These tours often include stops at community gardens or eco-conscious art installations, making your trip both educational and environmentally responsible.

Supporting Local Businesses & Ethical Tourism

Traveling responsibly means investing in the local economy and fostering cultural exchange. Every purchase, every meal, and every interaction can have a lasting impact on the community.

Local Markets & Artisans:

Explore vibrant markets like Cours Saleya and Marché de la Libération where you can buy fresh, locally sourced produce, handcrafted goods, and artisanal souvenirs. When you choose products made by local artisans, you're not just buying a keepsake—you're taking a piece of Nice's heritage home with you. This support helps maintain traditional crafts and ensures that local skills continue to flourish.

Ethical Dining:

Choose restaurants and cafés that source their ingredients locally and support sustainable practices. Many eateries in Nice emphasize seasonal menus featuring produce from nearby farms and local olive oils. Look for establishments that openly share their commitment to ethical sourcing and fair trade. By dining at these places, you contribute to a healthier food system and encourage culinary innovation rooted in regional traditions.

Community-Based Experiences:

Engage with cultural experiences that are run by locals. From cooking classes that teach you how to prepare traditional Niçoise dishes to guided tours of lesser-known neighborhoods, these experiences provide insights that go beyond surface-level tourism. They allow you to build genuine connections and foster mutual understanding between visitors and residents.

Responsible Shopping:

When shopping for souvenirs, opt for items that are handmade or produced locally. Whether it's a piece of pottery from a neighborhood artisan or a bottle of olive oil from a family-owned business, these purchases support sustainable livelihoods and help maintain the region's unique character.

Eco-Friendly Transport, Hotels & Dining Options

Eco-friendly accommodations and dining are essential elements of a sustainable travel experience. Nice offers several options that allow you to enjoy luxury and comfort while minimizing your environmental impact.

Eco-Friendly Hotels:

More hotels in Nice are embracing green practices—from energy-efficient lighting and solar panels to water-saving initiatives and waste reduction programs. Look for hotels that are certified green or have sustainability policies clearly displayed on their websites. Boutique hotels in neighborhoods like Cimiez and Le Port often have a local charm and focus on eco-friendly practices, providing guests with an authentic and responsible stay.

Sustainable Dining:

Choose restaurants that use organic, locally sourced ingredients and that minimize food waste. Many modern establishments in Nice now feature menus designed around sustainable practices. Some even participate in initiatives like donating surplus food to local charities. Whether you're indulging in a gourmet meal or enjoying a casual lunch at a bistro, ask your server about the restaurant's sourcing practices—it's a great conversation starter that underscores your commitment to ethical travel.

Green Transport Options:

If you plan on exploring beyond the city, consider renting a hybrid or electric car. Several rental companies in Nice now offer eco-friendly vehicles, and many provide detailed information on reducing your carbon footprint while driving along the picturesque coastal roads. Alternatively, regional train services in the French Riviera have been upgrading their fleets to include more sustainable, energy-efficient models, offering another great way to travel responsibly.

Eco-Friendly Amenities:

When preparing for your journey, bring reusable items like a water bottle, shopping bag, and coffee cup. Many establishments in Nice now offer discounts or incentives for guests who opt for sustainable practices. Small actions—like refusing single-use plastics or recycling properly—can add up to make a significant difference in preserving the beauty of the Riviera.

In Summary:

Sustainable and responsible travel in Nice is about making mindful choices that enrich your travel experience and contribute to the well-being of the local community and environment. From exploring the city on foot or by bike to supporting local markets and eco-friendly businesses, every decision you make helps maintain the charm and vitality of this beloved destination. Embrace these practices on your next visit to Nice, and you'll find that sustainable travel is not only good for the planet but also incredibly rewarding on a personal level.

16

AVOIDING TOURIST TRAPS & COMMON PITFALLS

Traveling to Nice is an exhilarating experience, but like any popular destination, it comes with its share of pitfalls that can derail your trip if you're not prepared. Over the years, I've seen how even the most seasoned travelers can fall prey to overpriced attractions, clever scams, and common mistakes that first-time visitors often make. Here's a detailed guide to help you navigate these challenges, ensuring that every moment of your stay in Nice is as authentic and enjoyable as possible.

What's Overrated & What's Worth Your Time?

In a city as vibrant as Nice, it's easy to get swept up in the hype of well-known attractions—but not everything that glitters is gold. Here are some insights to help you discern what's truly worth your time:

Overrated Spots:

Overcrowded Tourist Areas: While the Promenade des Anglais and the Old Town (Vieux Nice) are iconic, certain parts can become overwhelmingly crowded during peak season. Instead of sticking solely to the main thoroughfares, consider venturing into less trodden alleys or visiting early in the morning when the crowds are thinner.

Expensive Tourist Shops: Many souvenir stalls in the busiest parts of the city offer items that are mass-produced and marked up significantly for tourists. Rather than splurging on these, look for local markets like Cours Saleya or the Marché de la Libération for more authentic and reasonably priced keepsakes.

Worth Your Time:

Hidden Gems & Local Experiences: Seek out the lesser-known neighborhoods like Liberation or Le Port. These areas provide a more genuine taste of Niçois life, with quaint cafés, unique boutiques, and local art that tell the story of the city beyond the tourist brochures.

Cultural Experiences: Attend a local cooking class or a guided walking tour that dives into the history and traditions of Nice. These experiences offer lasting memories and genuine insights that large, commercial tours often miss.

Actionable Tip: Do a little research before your visit—look up local blogs, ask for recommendations on travel forums, and don't hesitate to ask locals for their favorite spots. Often, the best advice comes from those who call Nice home.

Common Scams & How to Stay Safe in Nice

Even in a beautiful and welcoming city like Nice, some individuals are eager to take advantage of unsuspecting travelers. Here are the most common scams and practical tips to keep you safe:

Pickpocketing:

What to Look Out For: In crowded places such as markets, public transportation, and major tourist sites, pickpockets often target distracted visitors.

How to Avoid It: Always keep your valuables in a secure, zipped bag, preferably worn across your body. Be mindful of your surroundings and avoid displaying expensive jewelry or gadgets.

Overpriced Services:

What to Look Out For: Some taxi drivers or street vendors might quote excessively high prices, especially if they sense you're unfamiliar with local rates.

How to Avoid It: Use official taxi services and insist on using the fixed fare when traveling from the airport to the city center. Familiarize yourself with the standard costs for meals, transportation, and attractions before you travel.

Fake Tour Guides:

What to Look Out For: Unlicensed individuals might approach you with "exclusive" tours or discounted tickets that turn out to be scams.

How to Avoid It: Always book tours through reputable agencies or trusted online platforms. Verify credentials if someone offers a tour on the spot.

Overcharging for Goods:

What to Look Out For: In markets and tourist-heavy areas, you might find vendors who initially quote a low price, only to dramatically increase it during the transaction.

How to Avoid It: Negotiate politely and agree on the price beforehand. Trust your instincts—if a deal seems too good or too complicated, it might be best to walk away.

Actionable Tip: Stay vigilant and maintain a healthy skepticism when approached by overly friendly strangers. A little caution goes a long way in protecting your wallet and ensuring your peace of mind.

Mistakes First-Time Visitors Make & How to Avoid Them

Every seasoned traveler has a few war stories about what they wish they'd done differently on their first trip. Here are some common pitfalls and tips to sidestep them:

Overpacking and Underpacking:

Mistake: Many first-timers either overpack, burdening themselves with unnecessary luggage, or underpack, finding themselves unprepared for Nice's variable weather.

Solution: Pack versatile clothing that can be layered for both warm, sunny days and cooler evenings. Remember, many attractions in Nice are walkable, so comfortable shoes are a must.

Failing to Research Local Customs:

Mistake: Not understanding local etiquette can lead to awkward situations—such as not greeting shopkeepers properly or misunderstanding dining etiquette.

Solution: A few basic French phrases go a long way. Familiarize yourself with local customs, such as greeting with a polite "Bonjour" and understanding that many restaurants include a service charge in the bill.

Over-Reliance on Tourist Information:

Mistake: Relying solely on mainstream travel guides can make your experience feel generic and overly commercialized.

Solution: Mix up your itinerary by incorporating advice from local blogs, conversation with residents, and personal exploration. Sometimes the best experiences are found off the beaten path.

Not Planning Enough Downtime:

Mistake: Trying to pack too many activities into one day can lead to burnout, leaving you exhausted and unable to enjoy the vibrant atmosphere of Nice.

Solution: Balance your schedule with a mix of planned excursions and leisurely time—maybe a relaxed afternoon at a beachfront café or a spontaneous stroll through a local park.

Actionable Tip: Make a flexible itinerary that includes "free time" slots. This not only allows for unexpected discoveries but also gives you the breathing room to enjoy each experience without feeling rushed.

In Conclusion:

Avoiding tourist traps and common pitfalls in Nice is all about staying informed, being prepared, and embracing a mindful approach to travel. By knowing what's overrated versus what's truly worthwhile, staying alert to common scams, and learning from the mistakes of others, you'll pave the way for a journey that's both enriching and worry-free. As you explore Nice, remember that the best adventures often come from the unexpected—so keep your wits about you, enjoy every moment, and let the true charm of the Riviera reveal itself in delightful, unanticipated ways.

17

PRACTICAL TRAVEL TIPS FOR A SMOOTH TRIP

When planning your adventure in Nice, a little preparation can transform your journey from stressful to seamless. Here, I've gathered practical tips—ranging from what to pack for the Mediterranean climate to digital resources—that will help you navigate every twist and turn of your trip with confidence and ease.

Packing Tips & Essentials for Nice's Climate

Nice is blessed with a Mediterranean climate that brings sunshine and gentle breezes for most of the year. However, the weather can shift subtly with the seasons, so packing smart is key.

Layer Up: Even in summer, early mornings and late evenings can be cool. Pack a light jacket or a cardigan that you can easily tie around your waist during the day. In spring and autumn, opt for versatile layers—think breathable t-shirts paired with a mid-weight sweater.

Sun Protection Essentials: The Riviera sun is generous. Bring a wide-brimmed hat, sunglasses with UV protection, and a high-SPF sunscreen. A reusable water bottle is also a must to stay hydrated as you explore the vibrant streets.

Comfortable Footwear: Nice is best experienced on foot—whether wandering through the cobblestone alleys of Vieux Nice or strolling along the Promenade des Anglais. Pack comfortable walking shoes that can handle uneven surfaces. If you plan to hike or explore off the beaten path, consider sturdy sneakers or light hiking shoes.

Beach Day Gear: Even though Nice's beaches are pebbly, you'll want a quick-dry towel, water shoes, and a swimsuit. A cover-up or a sarong is perfect for transitioning from the beach to a seaside café.

Adapters & Chargers: France uses type C and E plugs with a standard voltage of 230V. A universal travel adapter and portable power bank will keep your gadgets charged as you document your adventure.

Understanding Local Etiquette & Cultural Norms

Embracing local customs enriches your travel experience and fosters positive interactions with residents. Here are some essential etiquette tips for Nice:

Greetings: A friendly **"Bonjour" or "Bonsoir"** goes a long way. In many places, especially in smaller shops or cafés, greet the staff upon entering. A polite "Merci" and "Au revoir" are always appreciated.

Dining Etiquette: French mealtimes are sacrosanct. When dining out, wait to be seated and don't rush your meal. Tipping is typically modest—a few euros or rounding up the bill is common, as service charges are often included.

Dress Code: While Nice is generally relaxed, dressing smart-casual is a safe bet, especially in upscale dining or nightlife venues. Avoid overly casual attire (like flip-flops) when visiting religious sites or fine restaurants.

Language: Although many locals speak English, learning a few basic French phrases can make interactions smoother. Phrases such as "S'il vous plaît" (please) and "Merci beaucoup" (thank you very much) show respect for local culture.

Emergency Contacts, Health & Safety Information

Being prepared for the unexpected is crucial:

Emergency Numbers: In France, dial 112 for all emergencies (police, fire, or medical). Keep this number handy in your phone.

Health Care: Nice has excellent medical facilities. The Centre Hospitalier Universitaire de Nice (CHU Nice) is a well-regarded hospital. It's wise to have travel insurance that covers health emergencies and a small first-aid kit with essentials like pain relievers, band-aids, and any personal medications.

Local Safety: While Nice is generally safe, stay vigilant in crowded areas to guard against pickpocketing. Always secure your belongings, and if you ever feel uneasy, don't hesitate to seek assistance from local authorities.

Travel Insurance: Comprehensive travel insurance covering health, trip cancellations, and theft can save you from unexpected expenses and provide peace of mind.

Digital Traveler's Guide (Best Apps, WiFi, eSIMs & Useful Websites)

In today's digital age, the right apps and connectivity can make your trip smoother and more enriching:

Navigation & Transportation:

Google Maps or Citymapper: Essential for finding your way around the city on foot or via public transport.

Lignes d'Azur App: For real-time tram and bus schedules in Nice.

SNCF Connect: Useful if you plan to take trains to nearby destinations.

Language & Communication:

Duolingo: Brush up on basic French phrases before and during your trip.

Google Translate: Handy for translating menus or conversations on the go.

Connectivity:

Local eSIM Providers: Companies like Airalo and GigSky offer affordable eSIM options that let you stay connected without the hassle of swapping physical SIM cards.

WiFi Hotspots: Many cafés, hotels, and public spaces in Nice offer free WiFi. Apps like WiFi Map can help you locate them.

Travel & Event Planning:

TripAdvisor & Yelp: Great for restaurant reviews, local attractions, and real-time tips from fellow travelers.

Time Out Nice: A local guide for upcoming events, festivals, and must-visit spots.

Booking.com or Airbnb: For flexible accommodation options with user reviews to guide your choice.

Useful Websites:

Nice Tourism Official Site: Offers up-to-date information on events, transportation, and local tips.

Lignes d'Azur Official Site: For public transport updates and route planning.

By integrating these digital tools into your travel routine, you'll ensure that every moment of your stay in Nice is optimized, leaving you free to enjoy the experience without unnecessary stress.

18

ITINERARIES FOR EVERY TYPE OF TRAVELER

Nice, with its sun-drenched streets, rich history, and vibrant cultural tapestry, offers a wealth of experiences that can be tailored to any schedule or interest. Whether you have just a day to spare, a long weekend, or an entire week to immerse yourself in the magic of the French Riviera, these itineraries are designed to help you make the most of your visit. Here are some carefully crafted itineraries for every type of traveler, along with tips on how to customize your trip based on your interests.

24-Hour Itinerary: Maximizing a Short Visit

When time is of the essence, every minute counts. This 24-hour itinerary is for those who want to capture the essence of Nice in just one day.

Morning: A Fresh Start by the Sea

Sunrise on the Promenade des Anglais: Begin your day early with a serene walk along the Promenade des Anglais. The soft, early light casts a golden glow over the Mediterranean, setting the tone for your adventure.

Breakfast in Vieux Nice: Head into the Old Town for a classic French breakfast. Enjoy a buttery croissant and a strong espresso at a local boulangerie while people-watching in the charming narrow streets.

Quick Visit to Cours Saleya Market: Wander through the vibrant Cours Saleya Market. Absorb the sensory explosion of colors, smells, and sounds as you browse fresh produce, flowers, and artisanal goods.

Midday: Culture and Panoramic Views

Castle Hill (Colline du Château): Make your way to Castle Hill for breathtaking panoramic views of Nice. Whether you take the elevator or opt for the stairs, the vistas of the city, harbor, and coastline are a perfect backdrop for memorable photos.

Lunch with a View: Enjoy a light lunch at a café near Castle Hill or along the Promenade, savoring local specialties like a pan bagnat or a refreshing Niçoise salad.

Afternoon: Art and Historic Charm

Museum Stop: Dedicate some time to one of Nice's renowned museums. Choose between the Musée Matisse or the Marc Chagall Museum for a dose of art and culture.

Stroll Through Vieux Nice: Spend a couple of hours meandering through the labyrinthine streets of Old Town. Discover hidden alleyways, quaint boutiques, and local artisan shops, soaking in the authentic Niçois atmosphere.

Evening: Dine and Unwind

Dinner in a Traditional Niçoise Restaurant: As evening falls, treat yourself to dinner at a restaurant that specializes in local cuisine. Savor dishes like socca or pissaladière, paired with a glass of crisp rosé.

Nightcap on a Rooftop or Beachfront Lounge: End your day with a cocktail at a rooftop bar or a laid-back beachfront lounge. Revel in the dazzling city lights and the gentle sound of the sea, reflecting on a day well spent.

3-Day Itinerary: The Perfect Weekend in Nice

For those with a little more time, a three-day itinerary allows you to balance iconic landmarks with immersive local experiences.

Day 1 – Discovering the Heart of Nice

Morning: Start with breakfast in Vieux Nice. Explore the Cours Saleya Market, absorbing the local colors and flavors.

Enjoy a guided walking tour that introduces you to the city's history and architecture.

Afternoon: Climb or take the elevator up to Castle Hill for panoramic views.

Visit a museum of your choice—perhaps the Musée Matisse—to dive into the artistic legacy of Nice.

Evening: Dine at a mid-range restaurant in Old Town, and later, experience the local nightlife with a quiet drink at a charming café or a trendy bar.

Day 2 – Art, Culture & Local Flavors

Morning: Enjoy a leisurely breakfast at a café in the Carré d'Or district.

Visit the Musée Marc Chagall to appreciate the unique interplay of color and spirituality.

Afternoon: Explore lesser-known neighborhoods such as Liberation or Le Port, where local artisans and boutiques reveal a side of Nice away from the tourist crowds.

Savor lunch at a traditional bistro that offers authentic Niçoise fare.

Evening: Attend a local event, be it a live music performance or a small art exhibition.

Finish the day with a romantic dinner at a restaurant with a view of the sea.

Day 3 – A Day Trip Beyond Nice

Option 1 – Monaco: Take a short train ride to Monaco. Spend the day exploring the Casino de Monte-Carlo, the Prince's Palace, and the exotic gardens.

Option 2 – Antibes or Cannes: Choose a coastal excursion to Antibes or Cannes for a blend of art, beach relaxation, and boutique shopping.

Evening: Return to Nice for a relaxed dinner, perhaps at a beachfront restaurant where you can recount the day's adventures over a glass of local wine.

7-Day Itinerary: A Relaxed Yet Complete Experience

A full week in Nice lets you delve deeper into the city's charm while also exploring its surrounding gems. This itinerary is ideal for travelers who want to mix scheduled tours with spontaneous discoveries.

Day 1: Arrival and Orientation

Settle into your accommodation and take a gentle stroll along the Promenade des Anglais.

Enjoy a welcome dinner at a local restaurant to kickstart your culinary adventure.

Day 2: Old Town Immersion

Spend the entire day exploring Vieux Nice. Visit Cours Saleya, Place Rossetti, and the hidden alleys that house artisan shops.

Climb Castle Hill for sunset views, followed by dinner in one of the traditional eateries.

Day 3: Art and Culture

Dedicate a day to art: Visit the Musée Matisse, the Musée Marc Chagall, and the MAMAC.

Enjoy a gourmet lunch at a fine dining restaurant, and then spend your afternoon in the artistic ambiance of Cimiez.

Day 4: Local Experiences

Participate in a cooking class or a local workshop that delves into Niçoise cuisine.

Explore local markets and meet the artisans behind the region's famous products.

Have dinner at a bistro that focuses on farm-to-table dining.

Day 5: Outdoor Adventures

Venture out on a hiking trail such as the Sentier du Littoral for scenic coastal views.

Spend the afternoon at a private beach or try watersports for a bit of adventure.

End the day with a picnic on the beach as the sun sets.

Day 6: Day Trip Extravaganza

Choose a day trip: Visit Monaco for a taste of luxury, Cannes for its film festival allure, or Antibes for its art and history.

Enjoy a local lunch in your chosen destination before heading back to Nice.

Cap the day with a quiet dinner at a seaside café.

Day 7: Reflection and Leisure

Use your final day for leisurely exploration: Revisit your favorite spots, enjoy a spa treatment, or simply relax at a local café with a book.

Take time to shop for souvenirs in local markets, ensuring you leave with a piece of Nice's magic.

Enjoy a farewell dinner, perhaps with a rooftop view, to reflect on your week-long journey.

Customizing Your Trip Based on Interests

Every traveler is unique, and the beauty of Nice is that it offers a canvas you can tailor to your personal tastes and interests. Here are some tips for customizing your itinerary:

For Art Enthusiasts: Focus on the rich museum scene—allocate more time for the Musée Matisse, Musée Marc Chagall, and explore local galleries and street art tours in neighborhoods like Vieux Nice and Cimiez.

For Culinary Explorers: Integrate cooking classes, food market tours, and extended stops at renowned restaurants. Consider a dedicated day trip to nearby wineries or olive groves in Provence.

For Nature and Adventure Lovers: Increase the number of outdoor activities in your itinerary. Mix coastal hikes with cycling tours, and allocate a full day for watersports or exploring nearby natural parks.

For History Buffs: Incorporate guided historical tours of Vieux Nice, Castle Hill, and the Roman ruins in Cimiez. Seek out local heritage walks and visit smaller museums that delve into the city's past.

For Families: Prioritize family-friendly activities like visiting Parc Phoenix, interactive museums, and gentle beach days. Ensure that downtime is built into the schedule for rest and spontaneous play.

For the Budget Conscious: Look for free or low-cost activities such as exploring public beaches, wandering through local markets, and enjoying picnics in the park. Use public transport and consider affordable accommodations like hostels or budget hotels.

For Solo Travelers: Balance structured tours with ample free time to explore on your own. Join group activities or local meetups to connect with fellow travelers while still enjoying personal discovery.

Final Thought:

Customizing your itinerary in Nice is all about striking a balance between planned activities and spontaneous adventures. Whether you're ticking off a list of must-see attractions or wandering off the beaten path, every moment in Nice is an opportunity to create memories that are as unique as you are. Embrace the flexibility to adjust your plans along the way—sometimes the best experiences are those you never saw coming.

With these itineraries as your guide, you're well-equipped to design a journey through Nice that is perfectly in tune with your interests, pace, and dreams. Enjoy every moment on the French Riviera, where every street, beach, and corner of the city tells its own enchanting story.

19

FINAL THOUGHTS & INSIDER ADVICE

As your journey in Nice winds down, it's time to reflect on all the unforgettable moments and prepare for the next chapter of your adventure. Here are some final thoughts and insider tips to ensure you leave Nice with cherished memories—and the promise of a return.

A Local's Last Tips for the Best Experience

Imagine sitting at a quaint café in the heart of Vieux Nice, the aroma of fresh espresso mingling with the salt-tinged air of the Mediterranean. Here are some insider tips, as shared by locals who know the city best:

Embrace the Slow Pace: Don't rush your experience. Allow yourself to linger in a quiet square or savor a leisurely meal. Some of the most authentic moments in Nice are found in the pauses between activities—watching the world go by from a sunlit terrace, or striking up a conversation with a friendly local at a market stall.

Venture Off the Beaten Path: While the iconic landmarks are a must, make time to explore the hidden corners. Wander into lesser-known neighborhoods like Liberation or Le Port to discover local art, family-run eateries, and small boutiques. These unplanned discoveries often turn out to be the most rewarding parts of your trip.

Connect with the People: Engage with the locals—ask for recommendations, learn a few French phrases, and listen to their stories. Whether it's a chat with a seasoned baker at a traditional boulangerie or a conversation with a taxi driver who shares tales of the city's past, these interactions add a personal touch that no guidebook can capture.

Stay Open to Serendipity: Some of the best experiences in Nice come from spontaneity—a street performance in a hidden courtyard, an impromptu art exhibit, or a pop-up food stall offering a unique twist on traditional Niçoise dishes. Let your itinerary have some flexibility and allow the city to surprise you.

How to Leave Nice Without Regrets

Leaving a place as captivating as Nice can be bittersweet. Here's how to ensure that your departure is as smooth and satisfying as your arrival:

Savor Your Last Moments: On your final day, revisit your favorite spots—whether it's a quiet corner of the Promenade des Anglais at sunrise, a beloved café in Vieux Nice, or that panoramic view atop Castle Hill. Taking a few extra moments to soak it all in can turn your goodbye into a celebration of what you've experienced.

Reflect and Journal: Keep a travel journal or snap a few final photos that capture the essence of your journey. Write down what made your visit special—the unexpected kindness of a local, the flavors that danced on your palate, or the serenity of the Mediterranean sunset. This reflection not only helps preserve your memories but also creates a tangible reminder of the magic you found in Nice.

Plan for the Future: Don't let your trip end with your departure. Make note of the places you'd love to explore further, perhaps a return visit to a favorite restaurant or a day trip to a nearby village you missed. Leave your itinerary open-ended, knowing that Nice has a way of calling travelers back.

Stay Connected: Exchange contact details with any locals or fellow travelers who enriched your experience. Social media or email can serve as a bridge, keeping the spirit of Nice alive long after you've boarded your plane.

Why You'll Want to Return

Leaving Nice might be hard, but it's the kind of departure that leaves you yearning to come back. Here's why you'll find yourself planning your return even before you've left:

A City of Endless Discoveries: Every visit to Nice offers something new—whether it's a freshly uncovered street art installation, a seasonal festival that transforms the city, or a culinary discovery that delights your senses. Nice's dynamic blend of history, culture, and modern innovation ensures that no two visits are ever the same.

The Warmth of Local Hospitality: The genuine warmth and openness of the people in Nice create lasting impressions. The welcoming smiles, the shared stories, and the local pride are all part of what makes the city feel like home, even if just for a while.

A Perfect Blend of Relaxation and Adventure: Nice effortlessly combines the laid-back charm of a seaside retreat with the vibrancy of urban life. Whether you're unwinding on the pebbled shores, exploring bustling markets, or embarking on a scenic hike along the coast, the city offers the best of both worlds—a balance that keeps you coming back for more.

A Gateway to the French Riviera: Beyond its own allure, Nice is the ideal launchpad for further exploration of the French Riviera.

Each trip opens new possibilities for day trips and adventures in nearby glamorous cities and quaint villages, making it a perennial favorite for travelers who crave variety and depth.

Final Thoughts:

Nice is not just a destination—it's an experience that lingers in your heart long after you've left. By embracing its pace, connecting with its people, and allowing yourself to be enchanted by its hidden gems, you'll find that leaving Nice is only a temporary pause. With its promise of endless discoveries, heartfelt hospitality, and a perfect blend of relaxation and adventure, you'll always have a reason to return. Enjoy every moment, and until next time, au revoir!

20 FREQUENTLY ASKED QUESTIONS

Navigating a new destination can feel overwhelming, so here are some of the most commonly asked questions about traveling to Nice, along with detailed answers to help you plan a smooth and unforgettable trip.

1. What is the best time to visit Nice?

Nice enjoys a mild Mediterranean climate year-round, but your experience can vary greatly depending on when you visit.

Spring (March to May): Ideal for sightseeing and outdoor activities. Temperatures are pleasantly mild (around 12–20°C/54–68°F), and the city isn't as crowded. It's a perfect season for exploring the historic streets of Vieux Nice and taking leisurely strolls along the Promenade des Anglais.

Summer (June to August): This is peak season, with hot, sunny days (22–30°C/72–86°F) ideal for beach outings, water sports, and attending festivals like the Nice Jazz Festival. However, expect higher prices and larger crowds.

Autumn (September to November): A balanced season with comfortable temperatures (15–25°C/59–77°F) and fewer tourists. It's great for cultural tours and culinary experiences as local markets brim with seasonal produce.

Winter (December to February): Mild compared to other parts of Europe (6–15°C/43–59°F), making it a good time for budget travelers. The festive season brings events like the Nice Carnival, and the quieter streets offer a different, more intimate view of the city.

2. Do I need a visa or any special permits to visit Nice?

Nice is in France, which is part of the Schengen Area. Here's what you need to know:

For EU/EEA/Swiss Citizens: No visa is required—your valid national ID or passport is sufficient.

For Visa-Exempt Countries (e.g., USA, Canada, Australia, UK): You can visit visa-free for up to 90 days within a 180-day period. However, starting in mid-2025, you may need to apply for an ETIAS (European Travel Information and Authorization System) travel authorization before your trip.

For Other Nationalities: Travelers from countries not covered by visa exemptions will need to apply for a Schengen visa. Always check the latest requirements on the official French consulate or embassy website before booking your travel.

3. What currency is used, and how should I manage money in Nice?

Currency: The official currency is the Euro (€).

Payments: Credit and debit cards are widely accepted, especially in restaurants, shops, and hotels. It's advisable to carry some cash for smaller vendors, street markets, or places that do not accept cards.

Budgeting Tips: Public Transportation: A single ticket costs around €1.70, and multi-trip or day passes are economical if you plan to explore extensively.

Dining: Prices vary widely—budget eateries might charge €10–€15 per meal, whereas fine dining can be significantly higher.

Hidden Costs: Be mindful of tourist taxes in accommodations, ATM fees, and service charges in restaurants (often included in the bill).

4. How can I get around Nice?

Nice offers a variety of transportation options that cater to different needs and budgets:

Public Transportation: The city's tram and bus network (managed by Lignes d'Azur) is efficient and cost-effective. A single ticket or multi-trip cards work seamlessly across both modes of transport.

Walking & Biking: Nice is very walkable, especially in the Old Town and along the Promenade des Anglais. The city also has a public bike-share system (Vélo Bleu), and renting a bike can be a fun way to see the sights.

Taxis & Rideshares: Official taxis and services like Uber are available. Taxis operate on fixed rates for certain routes (e.g., €32 from the airport to the city center), but always confirm the fare beforehand.

Car Rentals: Renting a car is ideal if you plan day trips beyond the city. However, parking in central Nice can be challenging and expensive, so it's best to use a car only when venturing further afield.

5. What are some must-try Niçoise dishes and local specialties?

Nice is a culinary delight with flavors that reflect its Mediterranean heritage. Some local must-tries include:

Salade Niçoise: A refreshing salad featuring tomatoes, hard-boiled eggs, anchovies or tuna, olives, and green beans drizzled with olive oil.

Socca: A chickpea pancake that is crispy on the outside and soft on the inside—perfect as a snack or light meal.

Pan Bagnat: Essentially a Salade Niçoise in sandwich form, filled with all the flavors of the traditional salad.

Pissaladière: An onion tart topped with anchovies and olives, offering a savory taste of the region.

Local Sweets: Try delicacies like Tourte de Blettes (a unique Swiss chard pie) and candied fruits from local patisseries.

6. Is Nice family-friendly, and what activities are best for children?

Absolutely. Nice offers a range of family-friendly activities:

Parc Phoenix: A large botanical garden and zoo that delights children with interactive exhibits and diverse wildlife.

Beaches: While the beaches are pebbled, many are safe for families. Consider renting water shoes for comfort.

Museums: Some museums, like MAMAC, offer interactive exhibits that can engage younger visitors.

Old Town: The vibrant markets and narrow streets of Vieux Nice provide a sensory adventure for kids, though parental supervision is recommended in crowded areas.

7. How safe is Nice for travelers?

Nice is generally considered safe, but standard travel precautions are advisable:

Pickpocketing: Like many tourist destinations, crowded areas (markets, public transport, and tourist hotspots) can attract pickpockets. Keep your belongings secure and stay aware of your surroundings.

Emergency Contacts: In case of emergencies, dial 112 for immediate assistance (covers police, fire, and medical emergencies).

Local Advice: Respect local customs and etiquette to ensure a positive experience with residents. Use reputable services for tours, transportation, and accommodations.

8. What should I pack for a trip to Nice?

Packing efficiently can enhance your travel experience:

Clothing: Light layers are ideal—t-shirts, shorts, and sundresses for warm days, with a light jacket for cooler mornings and evenings. If you're visiting in spring or autumn, a mid-weight sweater is recommended.

Beach Essentials: Pack swimwear, water shoes (for pebbled beaches), a quick-dry towel, and a cover-up.

Sun Protection: Don't forget a hat, sunglasses, and high-SPF sunscreen, as the Mediterranean sun can be intense.

Electronics: Bring a universal adapter (France uses Type C/E plugs) and portable chargers. Consider an eSIM for hassle-free mobile connectivity.

9. How do I experience Nice like a local?

To truly immerse yourself in the Niçois way of life:

Engage with Locals: Learn a few basic French phrases and don't be afraid to ask for recommendations. Locals appreciate visitors who show genuine interest in their culture.

Venture Beyond Tourist Areas: Explore neighborhoods like Liberation or Le Port to experience authentic local life, with less crowded markets, quaint cafés, and unique boutiques.

Participate in Local Customs: Join in the pre-dinner "apéro" (drinks and snacks) or attend a local festival if the timing is right. These experiences offer insights that you won't find in guidebooks.

10. Are there sustainable travel options in Nice?

Yes, sustainable and responsible travel is increasingly supported in Nice:

Eco-Friendly Transport: Use the extensive public transport system, rent bikes, or simply walk to reduce your carbon footprint.

Green Accommodations: Many hotels and guesthouses in Nice now adhere to eco-friendly practices, from energy conservation to waste reduction.

Supporting Local: Buy locally-made products from markets and support ethical tourism by choosing locally operated tours and dining establishments that source their ingredients responsibly.

11. What digital tools and apps are recommended for traveling in Nice?

Staying connected and well-informed can make your trip smoother:

Navigation: Use Google Maps or Citymapper for real-time directions and public transport schedules.

Local Transport: The Lignes d'Azur app provides up-to-date tram and bus information.

Language: Duolingo and Google Translate can help you overcome language barriers.

Connectivity: Consider an eSIM from providers like Airalo or GigSky for affordable local data. WiFi Map is useful for locating free hotspots around the city.

Travel Planning: Websites like TripAdvisor, Time Out Nice, and the official Nice tourism site offer valuable insights into current events, must-see attractions, and local tips.

In Conclusion:

These FAQs cover a wide range of practical concerns and curiosities—from planning and packing to safety and local culture.

By preparing with these insights, you can focus on enjoying the myriad experiences that Nice has to offer, confident that you're ready to navigate its vibrant streets, stunning coastline, and rich cultural tapestry with ease. Happy travels, and may your adventure in Nice be as enriching as it is unforgettable!

SAFE TRAVELS AND ENJOY YOUR TIME IN THIS FASCINATING CITY!

Printed in Dunstable, United Kingdom